New England Time Line

by Ron McAdow

Second Edition

Nutshell Books
Southborough, Massachusetts

The purpose of *New England Time Line* is to provide a framework for understanding the region's history. It is intended as a reference for New England's important dates and as an aid to appreciation of the region's historic sites.

Second Edition

ISBN 1-880644-01-0

Printed in the United States of America

Library of Congress Catalog Card Number: 92-80179

Table of Contents

New England Time Line

1600s

1602 Gosnold explores New England coast
1607 Settlement attempted at Popham Beach, Maine

1616 Disease ravages Native Americans

1620 Pilgrims land at Plymouth
1623 English settlements in New Hampshire and Maine

1630 Boston founded

1636 Rhode Island founded
1637 Pequot War
1641 New Hampshire unites with Massachusetts

1662 Connecticut Colony chartered

1675-76
    King Philip's War

1689-97
    King William's War
1692 Witch trials at Salem

1700s

1702-13
    Queen Anne's War

1714 Vermont's first permanent white settlement

1735 Paul Revere born

1744 Abigail Adams born
1744-48
    King George's War

1754-63
    French and Indian War

1765 Stamp Act

1773 Boston Tea Party
1775 Battle of Lexington and Concord

1783 American Revolution ends
1788 U.S. Constitution adopted
1790 Pawtucket Mills begin production

1800s

1803 Emerson born;
       Middlesex Canal opens
1806 Boston and Hartford
       Turnpike

1820 Maine enters the Union

1825 Erie Canal opens

1835 Boston builds three
       railroads
1841 Community begins at
       Brook Farm
1844 Telegraph perfected

1850 Fugitive Slave Law

1861-65
       Civil War

1876 Telephone patented

1880 Southern New England
       deforested

1891 Basketball invented

1897 First Boston Marathon

1900s

1903 Baseball's first World
       Series

1917 American in World War I
1918 Flu epidemic

1920s
       Textile industry declines

1930 Half of region's farms have
       electricity
1934 First ski tow
1938 New England Hurricane
1941-45
       American in World War II

1955 Hurricanes Connie and
       Diane

1960s
       Suburbia sprawls through
       New England towns

1970 Vermont's Environmental
       Control Law

1980 Computer industry at peak
       of expansion

1992 Pequots open casino

5

Chronology

15,000

The most recent glacier retreats. At its height the ice covers all of New England, even the tallest mountains. Because much of the planet's water is locked into continental glaciers, oceans are lower during the Ice Age, coastal harbors are dry land, and mammoths graze on George's Bank. As the glacier melts, clay, sand, and gravel are released. The islands of Martha's Vineyard and Nantucket are deposited by the next to last glacier. They are called terminal moraines, and they mark the glacier's longest reach. Cape Cod is a terminal moraine of the last glacier. Huge lakes of glacial meltwater fill many New England river valleys, and sediments deposited on their floors will become the most productive of the region's soils.

9000+

Groups of Paleo-Indians hunt large mammals such as mastodon, bison, woodland caribou, and giant beaver. New England's climate resembles that of present-day northern Canada, and its vegetation gradually changes from tundra to northern forest.

9000-4000

New England is peopled by the Archaic Indians, hunter-gatherers who migrate between single-season camps and use a variety of vegetable and animal foods. In the estuary of the Charles River, Archaic Indians build a fish weir, the remains of which will be discovered during the construction of a Boston subway. The weir is a long fence of basketry supported by posts. The structure is

7

flooded at high tide, but it is dry when the tide is out; fish are trapped behind the basketry as the water recedes.

4000-2000

Archaeologists refer to this period as Transitional. The way of life remains that of hunter-gatherer, but people reside in multi-season villages. Judging by the quantity of artifacts they left behind, the inland population peaks during this time.

2700-1000

The Algonquians enter New England from the Midwest, bringing with them knowledge of pottery, the bow and arrow, and agriculture. The Algonquians become the dominant cultural influence, although it is unknown whether this takes place through gradual assimilation or by warfare. When the Europeans arrive, all American natives from the Maritime Provinces to North Carolina speak languages of the Eastern Algonquian family.

1000-500

In the Late Woodland Period, native farmers grow corn, beans, tobacco, and squash including pumpkins and zucchini. They make extensive use of fish, shellfish, and marine mammals; gather berries, nuts, seeds, and roots; and hunt deer, bear, beaver, raccoon, rabbit, and muskrat. Their homes are wigwams, which are framed with bent saplings and covered with mats or bark.

Canoes are the principal contribution of Native Americans to transportation. In northern New England birchbark canoes are made from single sheets of bark stripped from large paper birches. Southern craftsmen make dugout canoes from large trees. English settlers purchase canoes from the Indians and find them so useful they call them "water horses."

500   Contact between Native Americans and Europeans
follows the voyage of Columbus. The Abenaki (Dawn
Land People) populate northern New England. Vermont
and New Hampshire are the territory of the Western
Abenaki, although possession of Vermont is contested
by the fierce Iroquois of New York. Western Abenaki
tribes are the Ossippee, Pequawket, and Winnipe-
sauke. Eastern New Hampshire and all of Maine are
Eastern Abenaki, with separate tribes possessing
various river valleys—Maine's rivers are named by or
for the Abenaki groups that lived alongside them.

The Pennacook occupy southern New Hampshire
and include the Amoskeag, Nashua, Piscataqua,
Souhegan, and Squamscot tribes. The land that will be-
come Massachusetts is home to the Nipmuck,
Pawtucket, Massachusetts, and Wampanoag. Rhode
Island has mostly Narraganset but also Niantic,
Nipmuck, Pequot, and Wampanoag. Connecticut's na-
tives are Pequot, Mohegan, Tunxis, Housatonic, and
Wyachtonok.

Forest management by fire is practiced by the natives in much of New England. Annual burning of the
underbrush eases foot travel and encourages food-pro-
ducing plants such as strawberries, raspberries, and
blackberries without destroying the oaks, hickories, and
chestnuts that also generate valuable food for human
beings and their prey animals.

Years
A.D.

1492 **Columbus** finds the New World.

1498 **John Cabot,** hired to explore for King Henry VII, visits
the northern shores of North America. England's claim
to the continent is based on Cabot's "discovery."

1524 **Giovanni da Verrazano** sails along the Atlantic Coast
of North America. When he enters Narragansett Bay,
he is welcomed by a score of dugout canoes containing
hospitable natives who trade furs for glass jewelry.
After staying fifteen days with these Indians,
Verrazano continues up the coast, visiting Maine
before returning to Europe.

1530-1600
Although North America still has no permanent settlements, **Maine** has numerous temporary stations where
European sailors pause to trade for furs and to preserve
their fish by drying. Such stations are occupied for at
most a season and do not represent attempts at
colonization.

1580 **Massasoit,** sachem of the Wampanoag, is born about
this time. He is destined to become the protector and
benefactor of the Plymouth Colony.

1602 **Bartholomew Gosnold** explores New England's coast
in the ship *Concord*, seeking sassafras, because its fra-
grant roots are considered of medical value. Gosnold
sails along Maine and south to Cape Cod, which he
names for the excellent fishing he finds there. After
harvesting sassafras and visiting the Elizabeth Islands
and Martha's Vineyard, Gosnold returns to England
with an enthusiastic report on the commercial potential

10

of New England, supporting his claims with a profitable cargo.

1603 As a result of Gosnold's voyage, **Martin Pring** is sent to harvest two shiploads of sassafras. Pring ventures twenty miles up New Hampshire's Piscataqua River, then rounds Cape Ann and crosses Massachusetts Bay to the future site of Plymouth, where he spends seven weeks. His report of the bountiful crops of the natives encourages the belief that Massachusetts could support a colony.

1604 From his ship in Maine's Casco Bay, French explorer **Samuel de Champlain** sees the White Mountains of New Hampshire. In the following two years Champlain completes his map of the New England coast, visiting and charting the harbors that become Gloucester, Boston, and Plymouth.

   John Eliot is born in Hertfordshire, England. Eliot will devote much of his life to the welfare of Massachusetts Indians.

1605 **George Weymouth** explores the Maine coast for the English, investigating the Kennebec and St. George's Rivers.

1606 **James I** splits England's New World claims into Northern and Southern Virginia, which are soon to be separated by the Dutch colony of New Netherlands. Northern Virginia, which will come to be called New England, extends from the eastern end of Long Island to the northern tip of Nova Scotia.

   Maine's **Mount Desert Isle** is named by Samuel de Champlain, who observes that the summits of its rocky hills are without trees.

1607 Settlements are sent to both Virginias. Jamestown Colony is founded in the south. In the north, 120 adventurers attempt the **Sagadahoc Colony** at Popham Beach, Maine, near the mouth of the Kennebec River. The colonists build a small ship, the *Virginia*, the first vessel made in America by the English. A severe winter, a fire in the storehouse, and violent conflicts with the Indians prompt the survivors to return to England in 1608.

1608 Samuel de Champlain travels up the St. Lawrence River to **Quebec** and establishes the first permanent French colony in America. The next year he sails to Lake Champlain and explores Vermont.

1609 In July **Henry Hudson** spends a week in Maine's Penobscot Bay. The next month, his ship *Half Moon* touches Cape Cod, and in October he sails to the future site of Albany, New York, on the river that bears his name. Because Hudson's explorations are sponsored by the Netherlands, the Hudson River valley is claimed and colonized by the Dutch.

1612 **Anne Bradstreet**, destined to become America's first notable poet, is born Anne Dudley in England. She moves to America with her husband in 1630.

1614 **John Smith** explores New England and makes the best map to date of the coast from Penobscot Bay to Cape Cod, giving New England, Plymouth, Cape Ann, and the Charles River their English names. A second vessel on this expedition is commanded by Thomas Hunt, who kidnaps twenty native men at Plymouth and seven more at Cape Cod, and sells them as slaves in Spain. One of those enslaved is named Squanto, who travels from Spain to England and eventually to Newfoundland where, in 1618, he meets Thomas Dermer who is on his way to trade in Massachusetts. Dermer takes Squanto with him.

The history of the **Connecticut River** begins when Adriaen Block, a Dutch explorer, enters a river the natives call "Quaneh-ta-cut," claims the land around it, and trades with the Indians who bring furs down the river in bark canoes. Block and his company have lost their first ship to fire and have spent the winter on Manhattan Island building a new one, which they name the *Restless*.

1616-17

An **epidemic** destroys many of New England's native Americans. Between Saco Bay in Maine and Narragansett Bay in Rhode Island, the population of native coastal peoples is reduced from 100,000 in 1617 to 5,000 by 1619. The disease is suspected to have been a European childhood illness such as chicken pox or measles. English settlers will think that Divine Providence has removed the biggest obstacle to New England's settlement and has left cleared fields for their convenience.

1620 The *Mayflower* sails from England, landing at Provincetown in November, and moving on to Plymouth in late December. Of the 102 passengers on the *Mayflower*, 41 are Separatists, and only 27 of these are adults; the other 61 Pilgrims came to Plymouth for secular reasons. Their winter diet and shelter are inadequate, and only fifty Pilgrims survive until spring.

1621 The Pilgrims are pleasantly surprised to meet a bilingual Wampanoag named **Squanto** (see 1614). With Squanto as translator, discussions are held between the English leaders and Massasoit, the Wampanoag sachem, and peace is secured. Plymouth Colony's successful coexistence with the Wampanoags persuades

Puritans organizing in England that Massachusetts Bay is a feasible site for their colony.

1623 **New Hampshire's** first white settlement is a trading and fishing village established by David Thomson near the mouth of the Piscataqua River. By 1630 the principal settlement here is called Strawbery Banke, which in 1653 becomes Portsmouth.

English settlement at **Gloucester,** Massachusetts begins with a fishing colony sponsored by the Dorchester Company.

Kittery, Maine, is settled this year. In 1647 Kittery will become the first Maine town to incorporate.

1624 **William Blackstone** and others disembark at Plymouth. Blackstone (also spelled Blaxton) takes up residence on the side of a hill on a peninsula at the mouth of the Charles River, becoming the first Englishman to live on Beacon Hill. In 1631 Blackstone sells his holdings to the Puritans and moves to the river that is named after him, thus becoming the first white occupant of present-day Rhode Island. The orchard he plants will bear fruit for several centuries. Blackstone dies in 1675 a few days before the beginning of King Philip's War. One of the tales told of him is that when he was too old to travel on foot, Blackstone rode upon a bull he had trained for the purpose.

Plymouth Colony establishes trading posts at the future site of **Augusta,** Maine.

1626 The Gloucester colonists move to **Salem** to take up better farmland.

Puritan leaders in England form the **Massachusetts Bay Company** and are chartered to form a colony north of Plymouth.

1628   Autocratic **John Endicott** is sent to govern Salem. The original settlers soon move to Beverly.

1629   **Maine and New Hampshire** begin to take form with the division of the large tract of northern lands that had been granted to proprietors Fernando Gorges and John Mason. Maine goes to Gorges, and Mason receives land between the Merrimack and Piscataqua Rivers, which he calls New Hampshire after his native English county.

   The **Massachusetts Bay Colony** is chartered and granted all of the land from three miles south of the Charles River to three miles north of the Merrimack River, and west to the "South Sea," as the Pacific Ocean was then named. Six ships deliver 406 people to Salem. Some of these move on to establish Charlestown at the mouth of the Charles River.

1630   **Boston** is founded. John Winthrop, governor of the Massachusetts Bay Colony, lands at Salem but dislikes it and goes to Charlestown. Because Charlestown lacks a suitable water supply, Winthrop accepts William Blackstone's invitation to join him on the Shawmut Peninsula where there are good springs. The town established on Shawmut Peninsula is at first called Trimountain, but it is soon renamed Boston.

   When he sailed for the New World, Winthrop carried with him the **charter** of the Massachusetts Bay Colony, which was an indication that the administrative center of the new colony was to be in America, not in England.

   Fifteen hundred **Puritans** immigrate to Massachusetts this year, more than doubling the English population of New England. By the end of September five new towns have begun: Watertown, Roxbury, Dorchester, Medford, and Saugus.

1631 **John Eliot** arrives in Boston from England, and is made a minister at the church at Roxbury. The following year he marries Ann Mumford.

1632 **Edward Winslow** visits the Connecticut River. Massachusetts Bay colonists begin to think of expanding in this direction.

1633 The Dutch build a fort, the House of Hope, on the Connecticut River at the site of present-day Hartford, Connecticut. When Massachusetts Puritans sail past the fort's cannons to settle at **Windsor,** the Dutch hold their fire. Others from Massachusetts begin the town of **Wethersfield** on land they purchase from the sachem Sowheag. John Oldham and three others travel overland from Watertown, Massachusetts, to the Connecticut River.

   Gristmills powered by water are in operation in Massachusetts at Boston, Roxbury, and Saugus, and Cambridge is protected by a **log palisade** a mile and a half long.

1634 Voters from each Bay Colony town choose three representatives to the **Massachusetts General Court,** but voting is restricted to members of the Congregational church.

1635 **Roger Williams,** the minister at Salem, expresses his belief in religious freedom, and states that the English king cannot give away land owned and occupied by Indians. Williams is removed from his position, and is to be sent back to England, but he flees to Narragansett Bay and spends the winter with Massasoit and the Wampanoags.

   William Pynchon of Roxbury follows the Bay Path west until he reaches the Connecticut River at Agawam, where he founds a new town. In 1639

Agawam decides that it is part of Massachusetts and changes its name to Springfield.

1636 **Providence Plantation** is founded by Roger Williams and five companions on land purchased from the Narragansett Indians. The following year Williams helps Anne Hutchinson and her followers buy Aquidneck Island from the sachems Canonicus and Miantinomi. Like Williams, Hutchinson has been expelled from Massachusetts for expressing dissident religious views. On Aquidneck—soon to be known as Rhode Island—the town of Portsmouth is settled in 1637, and Newport in 1638. There are many wolves on the island, and arrangements are made with Miantinomi to have them hunted down. Despite the efforts of the Narragansetts, a decade later the English are still trying to rid Rhode Island of wolves.

Harvard College is founded in Cambridge, Massachusetts.

Proprietor **Fernando Gorges** establishes Maine's first government.

Thomas Hooker leads 100 followers from Cambridge to the Connecticut River, where they create Hartford on land deeded by the sachem Sequasson. At first it is called New Town, but soon it is named after Hertford, England, the home town of several important pioneers.

Connecticut Colony is formed by the towns of Hartford, Wethersfield, and Windsor.

1637 The **Pequot War** follows years of tension and several violent episodes. English from Connecticut, Massachusetts, and Plymouth, aided by Mohegans and Narragansetts, make a surprise attack on the Pequot town at Mystic. By setting fire to the houses and shooting those who flee the flames, they slaughter 700 people in less than an hour. The surviving Pequots attempt to withdraw to the Hudson River to join the Mohawks, but they are pursued and most are captured or killed. The Pequot leader, Sassacus, succeeds in reaching the Mohawks, only to be put to death by the people he hoped would protect him.

1638 **New Haven Colony** is founded by Massachusetts Puritans at a place on Long Island Sound called Quinnipiac by the natives. A large tract is bought from the sachem Momaguin for twelve cloth coats, twelve brass spoons, twelve hatchets, twenty-four knives, twelve porringers, and four cases of French knives and scissors.

The first **Baptist church** in America is founded by Roger Williams at Providence.

1639 The **Fundamental Orders of Connecticut** constitute organized government in that colony. Adopted at Hartford in January, the Fundamental Orders give citizenship to all who are accepted residents of their towns—they did not have to belong to the church, as they did in Massachusetts. The first governor of the colony is John Haynes, and one of the first actions of the colonial government is to standardize the size of bricks. The original towns of Connecticut Colony are Windsor, Wethersfield, and Hartford—the settlements at New Haven, Milford, and Guilford are independent.

1640 The **Great Migration** of Puritans takes place in the decade between 1630 and 1640. Twenty thousand immigrants come to New England before Puritans under Oliver Cromwell take over the government of England, eliminating their need for a safe haven. In the ensuing civil war, Charles I is arrested and is executed in 1649.

The *Bay Psalm Book*, the first book printed in America, is published in Cambridge by Stephen Daye.

Whitefield House is built in Guilford. It is Connecticut's oldest house, and thought to be the oldest stone house in New England.

1641 The colony of **New Hampshire** unites with Massachusetts and remains part of the Bay Colony until 1679.

New Haven Colony sets up a free school.

1642 **Massachusetts** requires parents to teach their children to read. After 1647 every Massachusetts town with more than fifty families must employ a schoolmaster to teach reading and writing.

Mount Washington, the highest of New Hampshire's White Mountains, is climbed by Darby Field. Indians guide Field to within eight miles of the summit, but stop there because they believed that they would die if they went to the mountain's top. Field found glistening stones on Mount Washington that he thought were diamonds, but they turned out to be quartz crystals.

1643 The **United Colonies of New England,** a confederation of Plymouth, Massachusetts, Connecticut, and New Haven, is established to unite English interests in opposition to their Dutch neighbors in New Netherlands. After New Netherlands becomes New York in 1664, the United Colonies has no more meetings.

1644 **Rhode Island** is chartered as a self-ruling colony with freedom of worship. In 1647, the independent colonies around Narragansett Bay unite under a charter that Roger Williams obtains in England. Connecticut and Massachusetts consider Rhode Island an aggregation of heretics, ignore it, and refuse to trade with it, so Rhode Island forms an economic relationship with the Dutch in New Netherlands.

1645 **Roxbury Latin School** is founded in Roxbury, Massachusetts.

The **Bay Colony** has twenty-three churches. Attendance and financial support are compulsory. Though Puritan doctrine softens during the second half of the century, Massachusetts and Connecticut are slow to separate church from state.

1646 **John Eliot** begins preaching to the Massachusetts Indians in their own tongue. Natick, the first and most enduring of the Indian towns Eliot founded, is established in 1651. A decade later, Eliot's translation of the Bible is published, using a version of written Algonquian that he has devised. By 1674, with the aid of funds raised in England, Eliot and his white and Indian colleagues have created fourteen towns of "praying Indians" throughout central Massachusetts.

The **Saugus Ironworks** is built under the guidance of Richard Leader. The initiator and financial organizer of the enterprise is John Winthrop Jr., well-educated son of the Massachusetts governor. After being refined from ore found in bogs, iron is made into bars of stock for use by blacksmiths, and is cast into kettles and firebacks (tablets of iron set at the back of fireplaces to reflect heat into the room).

1647 **Rhode Island** organizes its first government, officially named the "Incorporation of Providence Plantations in the Narraganset Bay in New England."

Heavy use of **tobacco** in Connecticut inspires a law stipulating that "no one under twenty years nor any other that hath not allreaddy accustomed himself to the Use thereof should take any Tobacco until he had a Certifcat from someone approved in Physicke that it is usefull for him."

1648 Corporal punishment is common in New England colonies, even for minor offenses. A Connecticut court rules as follows:

> The Court adjudgeth Peter Bussaker for his filthy and profane expressions (namely, that he hoped to meete some of the members of the church in hell ere long, and he did not but question that he should) to be committed to prison, there to be kept in safe custody, till the sermon, and then to stand the time thereof in the pillory, and after the sermon to be severely whipped.

1649 Wethersfield, Connecticut, builds its first ship. Shipbuilding will be an important industry in this town.

1650 Anne Bradstreet becomes America's first recognized poet when her *Tenth Muse* is published in London. Simon Bradstreet, her husband, is later the governor of Massachusetts Bay Colony. She lives in North Andover, Massachusetts, until her death in 1672. A sample stanza from her poem entitled "Contemplations:"

> When I behold the heavens as in their prime,
> And then the earth (though old) stil clad in green,
> The stones and trees, insensible of time,
> Nor age nor wrinkle on their front are seen;
> If winter come, and greeness then do fade,
> A Spring returns, and they more youthfull made;
> But Man grows old, lies down, remains where once he's laid.

1652 Pine tree shillings are made from Spanish dollars and other sources of metal at a Massachusetts mint operated by John Hull. Because the colonies are not permitted to manufacture money (minting is a royal prerogative), the shillings, although coined continuously until 1686, are all dated 1652, to give the impression that the minting ceased the year it began, at a time when the English throne was vacant.

1654 The **Dutch** are expelled from their fort at Hartford after decades of being crowded and insulted by their English neighbors.

1658 The first **Jews** arrive in Newport, Rhode Island, taking advantage of its religious toleration, as do many **Quakers**. The business activities of these two groups contribute to Newport's rise as a commercial center.

On **Cape Cod** a Quaker meeting is established in the town of Sandwich. Because of persecution its members help form a new settlement, in 1660, at Suckanesset, which will become Falmouth in 1694.

1659 **Quakers** are hanged in Boston. Mary Dyer is condemned to die with William Robinson and Marmaduke Stevenson, but Dyer is reprieved at the last minute and sent to Rhode Island. She returns the following spring and this time her execution is carried out. In 1660, the British monarch is restored, and the Puritans' persecution of Quakers is halted by Charles II, who sends a Quaker, Samuel Shattuck, as his emissary to the Massachusetts governor.

1660 The "**regicide**" judges (those who had signed the death-warrant of Charles I) arrive in Boston. Soon after the coronation of Charles II they flee to New Haven and Milford, Connecticut, and go into hiding. In 1664 they go to Hadley, Massachusetts, where the minister keeps two of them hidden in his house for many years.

Celebration of **Christmas** is forbidden by law in Massachusetts, but New England Puritanism does not frown on alcohol. Cider and beer are served with every meal including breakfast, and both men and women use tobacco.

1661 **Massasoit** dies, and his son Metacomet, called Philip by the English, becomes sachem of the Wampanoag.

Connecticut's General Court begins meeting in Hartford in the upper room of Jeremy Adams's tavern, which serves as the legislative chamber for half a century—money is voted to build a state house in 1719. The General Court decides to acknowledge allegiance to Charles II and to send John Winthrop, Jr. to attempt to obtain a colonial charter.

1662   Winthrop succeeds in obtaining a **charter** for Connecticut Colony, giving it land seventy-three miles wide from Narragansett Bay to the Pacific Ocean, bounds that include New Haven and Rhode Island. New Haven Colony has little desire to join Connecticut, but because the prospect of being swept into New York is clearly the greater evil, New Haven merges with Connecticut in December of 1664.

        At **Portsmouth,** New Hampshire, a cage is constructed for the display of miscreants "such as sleep or take tobacco on the Lord's Day out of the meeting in the time of public service."

1663   Charles II grants **Rhode Island** a new charter that further clarifies the colony's policy of free thought: "no person within the colony, at any time hereafter shall be in any wise molested, punished, disquieted, or called in question for any difference of opinion in matters of religion."

1664   **New Netherland** is seized by England's Charles II, who sends four ships to force Dutch capitulation. Charles gives the area to his brother, the Duke of York. New Netherland and its principal town, New Amsterdam, are renamed New York. No effort is made to impose the English language or religion on the Dutch.

1666 Settlement of present-day **Vermont** begins when the French erect a fort on Isle La Motte in Lake Champlain.

1672 **Roger Williams**, age seventy-three, rows a boat all day to reach Newport from Providence, because he is determined to join in a debate with some Quakers.

1674 **Wearing silk** and having long hair are the offenses for which thirty young Connecticut men are arrested this year.

1675 **King Philip's War** begins. The Wampanoag sachem leads an attempt to extinguish the Massachusetts Bay Colony. Hostilities commence in July with Indian attacks on Swansea and Mendon. Though whites outnumber the Indians, in the fall of 1675 the English are forced to face the possibility of their annihilation as the towns of Brookfield, Dartmouth, Deerfield, Groton, Lancaster, Mendon, Middleborough, Northfield, Simsbury, Warwick, Wickford, Worcester, and Wrentham are destroyed. The Great Swamp Fight takes place in December when troops from the Puritan colonies invade neutral Rhode Island to drive the Narragansetts from their homes.

1676 The Indians have the advantage during the winter and spring, but their efforts weaken as they deplete the supplies of the villages they have captured and their own towns and crops are burned by the whites. Most of Philip's warriors disperse or surrender during the summer, and Philip is killed in August. Massachusetts and Plymouth have lost 600 people—a tenth of the white male population—and fifty towns. The Indian losses are about 3000, approximately one-third of their population. Most Indian captives are executed or sold into slavery in the West Indies. Some of the surviving Indians flee to Maine and incite the local Abenakis to destroy white settlements at Casco, Pemaquid, Cape Neddick, Black Point, and Arrowsic.

Despite the fear and tension of war, there is **romance** on Cape Cod. A young woman named Hetty Shepard writes in her diary:

> March 20. Sabbath at meeting. Mr. Willard spoke to the second commandment. Mr. Eliot prayed. While we were ceasing for half an hour, I saw Samuel Checkly and smiled; this was not the time to trifle and I repented, especially as he looked at me so many times after that I found my mind wandering from the psalm. And afterwards, when the Biskets, Beer, Cider, and Wine were distributed he whispered to me that he would rather serve me than the elders, which was a wicked thing to say, and I felt myself to blame.

Samuel Checkly and Hetty Shepard marry the following year.

1679 **New Hampshire** separates from Massachusetts and is established as a royal colony, with Portsmouth as its capital.

Wild turkeys, plentiful when the English arrived in Massachusetts, are by this time becoming rare. Soon they are eliminated from the region, but are restored in the 1970s.

1685 In an attempt to tighten control of the colonies, James II appoints **Sir Edmund Andros** governor of the newly organized "Dominion of New England." There is bitter opposition within the colonies because they have become accustomed to a large degree of self-rule.

1686 Andros arrives in Boston in the frigate *Kingfisher*, with a guard of British soldiers, to be captain-general and governor-in-chief of New England.

The **Huguenots** are banished by Louis XIV. About 200,000 Protestants leave France, many of whom come to New England.

1687 According to Connecticut legend, Governor Andros demands that the colony's charter be surrendered at a meeting in Hartford. At a signal, all of the candles are extinguished, and when they are relit, the Charter is gone! It is hidden in the hollow of a large tree celebrated thereafter as the **Charter Oak**, which finally blows down in 1856. Andros takes power anyway.

1688 In England's "**Glorious Revolution,**" James II is deposed and William and Mary are enthroned.

The **Abenaki Indians** revolt in Maine. Pemaquid is abandoned, and Dover, New Hampshire, is sacked.

1689 News of the "Glorious Revolution" reaches New England. Colonists gleefully arrest Governor Andros and put an end to the Dominion of New England. Connecticut produces its charter from hiding and resumes its previous mode of government. One effect of the Dominion of New England is the permanent reduction of the power of the Puritan oligarchy.

The **French and Indian Wars** begin, a prolonged struggle between England and France. This conflict has four parts: King William's War, Queen Anne's War, King George's War, and the French and Indian War.

1690 **Portland** is destroyed by French and Indians. By the next year the only Maine towns still standing are Wells, Kittery, York and settlements on the Isles of Shoals.

1691 **Plymouth** is incorporated into the Massachusetts Bay Colony. The charter of their union provides for "liberty of conscience to all Christians, except Papists."

Massachusetts also absorbs **Maine**, having over the years purchased the holdings of its proprietors. Until it becomes a state in 1820, Maine remains part of Massachusetts.

1692 **Witch trials** at Salem result in the execution by hanging of fourteen women and five men. Another man dies while authorities attempt to force a confession by having him "pressed" with stones.

1696 In giving **Colonel Thomas Howe** permission to keep an inn at Marlborough, Massachusetts, the town stipulates that "he shall not suffer to have any playing at cards, dice, tally, bowls, ninepins, billiards, or any other unlawful game or games in his said house...nor shall he entertain any persons of jolly conversation or given to tippling."

1697 During an Indian attack on Haverhill, Massachusetts, a woman named **Hannah Dustin** is taken prisoner. A few nights later, with the help of another woman and a young boy, Dustin kills ten of her captors as they sleep, and makes good her escape.
The **Peace of Ryswick** ends King William's War.
Salem witch trial judge **Samuel Sewall** publicly confesses his errors at Boston's South Church.

1698 Because numerous **pirates** are based in New England, the British government orders the colonial governments to repress them. Captain Kidd is arrested in Boston and sent to England, where he is executed in 1700.

1700s
The **Narragansett Pacer**, a breed of saddle horse, is developed on Rhode Island plantations.

1701 **Yale College** is founded. The first commencement is held at Saybrook, Connecticut, but in 1716 the college moves to New Haven. Originally called the Collegiate School, in 1718 it takes the name of Elihu Yale, a New Haven native, governor of Britain's East India Company, and principal benefactor of the college.

1702 **Queen Anne's War** begins. Abenaki and French attack the English outposts in Maine.

1704 **Deerfield, Massachusetts** is attacked by French and Indians. John Williams and most of his large family are captured or killed. His seven-year-old daughter Eunice is taken to Canada, where she is raised as a Catholic and marries an Iroquois. Though she comes home for a visit in 1740, she astonishes her family by choosing to return to her life in Canada.

1712 The first **sperm whale** is brought to Nantucket and found to contain a large quantity of valuable oil that can be burned in lamps. Whaling ships seeking sperm whales begin making longer voyages into deep water, and by 1730 they are venturing to Brazil and to the arctic.

1713 A peace treaty between Great Britain and France ends Queen Anne's War and inaugurates expansion into western and northern New England. Nova Scotia and Newfoundland become British colonies.
  America's first **schooner** is built in Gloucester, Massachusetts.

1714 **Fort Dummer,** Vermont's first permanent white settlement, is built near present-day Brattleboro to protect Massachusetts' frontier.

1715-90

Most New England houses built in this period are **Georgian,** an architectural style typified by symmetrical designs with the door in the center and windows evenly spaced on either side. Often there are tall, slender windows called lights beside the door. Georgian house styles remain popular well into the 1800s.

1716 A house is built in Sudbury, Massachusetts, that will become famous as the setting of Longfellow's *Tales of a Wayside Inn* (see 1807).

Wigs have became very fashionable in New England despite the objections of Puritan preachers.

North America's first **lighthouse** is built in Boston Harbor on Little Brewster Island.

1719 Scotch-Irish immigrants settle in **Londonderry**, New Hampshire, where they introduce the manufacture of linen and the cultivation of potatoes.

April Fool's Day is scorned by Boston's Judge Samuel Sewall, who writes in his diary:

> April 1. In the morning I dehorted Sam Hirst and Grindell Rawson from playing Idle tricks because 'twas the first of April: They were the greatest fools that did so. New England men came hither to avoid anniversary days, the keeping of them such as 25th of December.

Strict Congregationalists resist the temptations of Christmas for many more years; it is not celebrated throughout New England until the time of the Civil War.

1721 New England suffers from a **smallpox epidemic.** Boston surgeon Zabdiel Boylston experiments with inoculation, but not until 1796 is there an effective vaccine. Boylston's inoculations are controversial, but he receives the support of influential minister Cotton

Mather, who later writes America's first medical treatise.

1722 **Billiards** can be played in a pub in Charlestown, Massachusetts.

1728 The *Boston News Letter* of November 18 prints its estimate of the daily expenses of food:

Breakfast 1d. a Pint of Milk 2d 3d

Dinner. Pudding Bread meat Roots Pickles Vinegar Salt and Cheese... 9d

(In this article of the Dinner I would include all the Raisins Currants Suet Flour Eggs Cranberries Apples & where there are children all their Intermeal Eating)

Supper As the Breakfast.. 3d

Small Beer for the Whole Day 1 1/2d

For one Person a Day in all 1s. 4 1/2d

Twelve pence (d) make a shilling (s.), and twenty shillings make a pound.

1729 The **South Meeting House** is constructed in Boston. Phyllis Wheatley, America's first published African-American poet, worships here.

1730 Boston's **Long Wharf** extends 2000 feet from State Street to deep water.

1732 **Iron ore** is discovered at Salisbury, Connecticut. In the ensuing decades several ironworks begin operations in this area. Cannons will be cast here for the American Revolution and to arm the *Constitution* and other warships.

1735 **Paul Revere** is born in Boston.

1740s

A religious revival called the **Great Awakening** is inspired by Jonathan Edwards of South Windsor, Connecticut, whose preaching emphasizes a wrathful God and the punishment of sinners. Those who oppose this movement seek milder doctrines in independent "New Light" churches or join the comparatively democratic Baptists—Baptist women vote on church affairs.

1741 The boundary between Massachusetts and New Hampshire is surveyed.

1744 **Abigail Adams** is born Abigail Smith in Weymouth, Massachustts, the daughter of a Congregational minister.

King George's War begins, the third in the series of conflicts known collectively as the French and Indian Wars.

1745 The French fortess at **Louisbourg** on Cape Breton Island is attacked by English colonists. The action is instigated by William Vaughn of Damariscotta, Maine, and led by William Pepperell of Kittery. Positioned to control access to Canada, Louisbourg is the New World headquarters of the French Navy. The fortress is considered impregnable because it is protected on three sides by deep water and by a marsh on the fourth side. The Yankees capture the guns of a small companion fort and, by heroic labors, build a causeway into the marsh. The guns are dragged onto the causeway and fire upon the city. Running low on supplies and suffering from the cannonade, Louisbourg capitulates, giving colonial New England its paramount military triumph. Pepperell is made a baronet by the British, who are quite surprised at the success of the untrained Yankees.

1748 The **Treaty of Aix-la-Chapelle** ends King George's War. A provision of the treaty returns Louisbourg to the French, which enrages New Englanders.

1751 America's first **snuff mill** is erected at Narragansett, Rhode Island.

1754 The **French and Indian War begins.** As a result of this war, France loses its New World colonies, Britain accumulates a debt, and American military leaders such as George Washington gain combat experience.

    Joshua Moor dies and leaves his house in Lebanon, Connecticut, to Reverend Eleazer Wheelock, the town's pastor, who has been preaching to Indians since 1735. Wheelock gathers Delaware, Mohegan, and Mohawk students and forms Moor's Indian Charity School, which moves to Hanover, New Hampshire, in 1770 and eventually becomes Dartmouth College.

    An **almanac** published in Connecticut by Roger Sherman predicts this weather for December: "Freezing cold weather, after which comes a storm of snow, but how long after I don't say."

1755 The French residents of **Acadia**, which the British call Nova Scotia, are expelled by the British. Some of the French move to Louisiana, where their descendants will be known as Cajuns, derived from Acadians. Others disperse through New England.

1756 **Paul Revere** serves briefly in the French and Indian War. Upon his return to Boston he marries Sarah Orne and takes up silversmithing, which is his father's trade.

1759 **Rogers' Rangers** massacre of Indians at St. Francis, Quebec, secures northern New England for settlements from the British colonies.

1760-63
New Hampshire's **Governor Benning Wentworth** makes 138 land grants in present-day Vermont, which is subsequently known as the Hampshire Grants. The first town to be chartered is called Bennington.

1763 The **Treaty of Paris** ends the French and Indian Wars and gives Britain control of all of Canada and all land east of the Mississippi River.

    Moses Brown founds Rhode Island College. In 1770 the college will move to Providence, and in 1804 will change its name to Brown.

    Newport's **Touro Synagogue** is dedicated this year. The oldest continuously operating synagogue building in North America, it is named after Judah Touro, a successful merchant who contributed funds for construction.

1764 Britain places **Vermont** under the control of New York by declaring the Connecticut River to be the boundary between New York and New Hampshire. New York attempts to expel settlers from New Hampshire who refuse to re-purchase their land, thus initiating thirteen years of tension. The Green Mountain Boys form in 1770 to defend what they regard as their property rights. In 1774 the governor of New York offers a reward of fifty pounds apiece for the capture of leaders of the Green Mountain Boys.

    Abigail Smith marries John Adams. John Quincy Adams, the second of their six children, will become the sixth president of the United States.

1765 Attempting to raise money to pay debts from the French and Indian War, Britain passes a **Stamp Act** requiring Americans to purchase stamps for legal and business papers, pamphlets, and newspapers.

Chocolate is first made in North America at a mill on the Neponset River in Massachusetts.

1766 In Providence, the **Daughters of Liberty** form to oppose the Stamp Act. To reduce imports from Britain, they spin wool at all-day meetings. The president and first graduating class of Rhode Island College all wear homespun clothing to commencement to underline their admiration of the Daughters of Liberty. Such colonial protests prompt repeal of the Stamp Act, but Britain continues attempts to tax the colonies.

1767 Parliament passes the **Townshend Acts,** which place a tax on glass, paper, paints, and tea.

1768 British troops are sent to Boston, which has become a hotbed of resistance to the authority of the Mother Country. Throughout New England, the schism between "Patriots" and "Loyalists" deepens.

Paul Revere places this advertisement in the *Boston Evening Post*:

> Whereas many Persons are so unfortunate as to lose their Fore Teeth by Accident or Otherways to their great Detriment not only in looks but in speaking both in public and private. This is to inform all such that they can have them replaced with Artificial Ones that look as well as the Natural and answer the End of Speaking by Paul Revere Goldsmith near the head of Dr. Clarkes wharf.

1769 The British ship *Liberty* is burned at a dock in Newport.

1770 The **Boston Massacre.** Under attack by a stone-throwing mob, British soldiers open fire, killing three people. Even though they are tried in Boston, the soldiers, defended in court by John Adams, are found to have acted in self-defense. Nevertheless, Patriots generate propaganda from the incident. A Boston newspaper prints Paul Revere's engraving of the shooting of "unarmed" citizens. The British government cancels all of the Townshend Act taxes except for a small levy on tea.

1772 The *Gaspee* affair. The *Gaspee* is a revenue cutter that has been quite successful in thwarting smuggling in Narragansett Bay until it runs aground near Providence, thus giving a mob of locals the chance to beat up the crew and burn their ship. British officials do not succeed in arresting the offenders, but their effort to do so deepens the rift between Britain and the American colonies and leads to the establishment of Committees of Correspondence, which become an important channel of communication between the colonies.

1773 The **Boston Tea Party.** The night before three ships of British-owned tea are to be unloaded, Patriot leader Sam Adams holds a public meeting at the Old South Meeting House. On Adams's cue, "This meeting can do nothing more to save the country," the Sons of Liberty go to the wharf and dump 342 chests of tea into the harbor. One of the participants is Paul Revere.

1774 Parliament passes the **Intolerable Acts** in response to the Boston Tea Party. Britain closes the port of Boston and suspends the Massachusetts legislature, placing the colony under the rule of General Gage, who arrives in Boston with additional troops. The General's power is effective only within the city; the rest of the colony forms its own government. Companies of Patriot militia begin training in towns throughout New England.

The colonies prepare for united action by holding a
Continental Congress; John Adams represents
Massachusetts.

In New Hampshire, Patriot activists called Sons of
Liberty are warned by Paul Revere that British ships
are coming to take military supplies stored at **Fort
William and Mary** in Portsmouth Harbor. The colonists
surprise the fort's small garrison and take ninety-nine
kegs of gunpowder for use in the forthcoming war.

Patriots in **York**, Maine have their own tea party,
but instead of dumping the tea into salt water, they
burn it. The following spring another tea-burning takes
place in Providence.

Shaker leader Ann Lee arrives from England and
begins converting Americans to her religious sect. Because Ann Lee is British and advocates pacifism, the
Shakers encounter fierce resistance in their early years,
but they persist in advocating their celibate, communal
way of life and by 1800 establish eleven communities in
New York and New England with a combined population of 1373. In the twentieth century Shaker numbers
decline, and at this writing their only active community
is at Sabbathday Lake in Maine.

1775 The **American Revolution** begins with the Battle of
Lexington and Concord. British troops stationed in
Boston under the command of General Gage are dis-
patched to seize Patriot munitions stored in Concord.
Patriot leaders have anticipated this move, and com-
panies of local militia called Minute Men have trained
to meet such an emergency. When the British troop
movement begins on the night of April 18, a young
Patriot from Boston, William Dawes, slips by the
British sentries and rides through Roxbury, Brookline,
Cambridge, and Menotomy (Arlington) on his way to
Lexington, spreading the alarm as he goes.

Two lanterns are hung in the steeple of Christ
Church (now called Old North) to signal Patriots in
Charlestown that the redcoats are moving by boat up
the river rather than marching on Boston Neck. Mean-
while, Paul Revere is rowed across the mouth of the
Charles River and is lent a horse so that he can ride to
Lexington. The bell in the Lexington meetinghouse
calls out the Minute Men. Revere is stopped by a
British patrol, but Dr. Samuel Prescott carries the
warning to Concord.

The British troops disembark at East Cambridge, in
the early hours of April 19, and after a long delay begin
their march through what are now Somerville and
Arlington. The column is confronted at dawn on
Lexington Green by the town's Minute Men, under
Captain Parker, who orders his seventy-seven men to
"Stand your ground! Don't fire unless fired upon! But if
they mean to have a war, let it begin here!"

The British commander, Major Pitcairn, shouts to
the Minute Men, "Lay down your arms, you damned
rebels and disperse!" Seeing his men outnumbered ten
to one, Captain Parker is willing to withdraw, but there
is a gunshot—no one knows who fired it—and then a
British volley kills eight Patriots.

The British continue to Concord and search for arms,
most of which have been hidden. A detachment is sent
to the west of the village to guard the North Bridge
over the Concord River. When Minute Men on the high
ground across the river see smoke from the village center, they believe that the British are setting fire to the
town and they decide to force their way across the
bridge. The British guards fire from the bridge and the
Minute Men return fire. There are casualties on both
sides, and the surviving British retreat to the center of
town.

Minute Men stream toward Concord from all direc-
tions. By the time the scarlet-clad column begins its

withdrawal toward Boston, it is surrounded by hostile colonial militia. For the most part the Americans are held out of musket range of the column by British flankers, but where they can hold positions near the road they take a heavy toll. By the time they have reached Charlestown the British have lost 73 dead and 174 wounded. The Americans lose 49 dead and 40 wounded.

The British retreat into Boston, and the Americans lay siege to the city.

In May, **Fort Ticonderoga** is captured by Vermont's Green Mountain Boys led by Ethan Allan and by Benedict Arnold, a native of Norwich, Connecticut. The following winter, fifty cannon from Ticonderoga are transported over the snow to Boston (see 1776).

The **Battle of Bunker Hill** takes place on June 17 after Patriots occupy high ground that threatens Boston, forcing the British to cross the Charles River to dislodge them. The Redcoats are eventually successful in capturing the hill, but they suffer fearful casualties in doing so, and the Americans' will to fight is demonstrated beyond doubt. To retaliate for sniper fire from the town, the British burn Charlestown.

Patriot forces are adopted by the Continental Congress, and in July **George Washington** takes command of the Continental Army in Cambridge.

Benedict Arnold leads American troops up the Kennebec River and across Maine to attempt the capture of Quebec. The attack is ill-conceived; the commanders have underestimated the difficulties of the journey. The force reaches its destination in no condition to fight. Though reinforced by sea, Arnold is defeated.

In October, the British navy destroys Falmouth (now Portland, Maine) with warship guns. The British commander aims his fire over the buildings until most residents have withdrawn. Tavernkeeper Alice Greely stays with her establishment and puts out fires as they start; hers is the only public building to survive.

1776 **Fifty cannon** from Fort Ticonderoga are moved over snow by draft animals and presented to General Washington in Cambridge. In March, Washington places these cannon on Dorchester Heights, from which they command Boston. The British are allowed to depart in safety with the proviso that they do not set fire to the town. Most of Boston's Loyalists leave with the troops.

Abigail Adams writes to her husband at Philadelphia:

> In the new Code of Laws which I suppose it will be necessary for you to make I desire you would remember the Ladies, and be more generous and favorable to them than your ancestors... If particular care and attention is not paid to the ladies we are determined to foment a rebellion, and will not hold ourselves bound by any laws in which we have no voice or representation.

Adams and the other fore*fathers* disregard this advice.

On the fourth of July the **Declaration of Independence** is proclaimed by the Continental Congress.

Newport, Rhode Island, is occupied by British troops until 1779.

1777 New Hampshire troops win the **Battle of Bennington,** which is fought west of the town, in New York. This fight leads to the important American victory at Saratoga. The American commander at Bennington is General John Stark (1728-1822), who had been a captive of the Abenaki for part of his youth, and from whom he had learned his wilderness skills. Speaking to his men before the battle, Stark said, "There are the redcoats, and they are ours, or this night Molly Stark sleeps a widow." Stark Peaks and the town of Stark, New Hampshire, bear the General's name.

Vermont declares itself an independent republic and establishes its own coins and units of weight and measure.

Abigail Adam writes of wartime deprivations:

> There is a great scarcity of Sugar and coffee, articles which the female part of the State is very loath to give up, especially whilst they consider the great scarcity occasioned by the merchants having secreted a large quantity...It was rumored that an eminent stingy wealthy merchant (who is a bachelor) had a hogshead of coffee in his store which he refused to sell the committee under six shillings per pound. A number of females, some say a hundred, some say more, assembled with a cart and trunks, marched down to the warehouse and demanded the keys which he refused to deliver. Upon which one of them seized him by his neck and tossed him into the cart. Upon his finding no quarter he delivered the keys when they tipped up the cart and discharged him; then opened the warehouse, hoisted out the coffee themselves, put [it] into the trunks and drove off...A large concourse of men stood amazed, silent spectators of the whole transaction.

The sloop-of-war *Ranger* is launched at Kittery, Maine, and placed under command of **John Paul Jones**. *Ranger* hurries to France with word of the American victory at Saratoga, which helps persuade France to support the cause of American independence.

1778 **Phillips Academy** is established in Andover, Massachusetts. Another Phillips Academy opens three years later in Exeter, New Hampshire.

1779 The **Penobscot Expedition**, an attempt to recapture territory in Maine held by the British, ends in failure, and Paul Revere's conduct as commander of artillery is called into question.

1780 **Massachusetts** adopts a constitution written by John Adams. Its bicameral legislature and system of three governmental branches with countervailing powers is largely imitated in the federal constitution written eight years later.

May 19 is a phenomenally **dark day** in New England—candles are in use at midday, and chickens go to roost. Heavy smoke from western forest fires is thought to have been the cause.

1780-86

Land between the Appalachians and the Mississipi has been claimed by Connecticut and Massachusetts in accordance with the terms of their colonial charters. During these years the claims are surrendered, but Connecticut retains its "Western Reserve," most of which will be sold to benefit public education in the state.

1781 Shaker founder **Ann Lee** and several followers come to Massachusetts and start a Shaker community in the town of Harvard.

1783 **Noah Webster** of West Hartford, Connecticut, publishes his first spelling book, the *Grammatical Institute*, spawning a craze for spelling bees, which become a popular recreation in much of New England. The *American Dictionary of the English Language* will appear in 1828, the product of twenty-six years of labor. So many copies of Webster's books on spelling and grammar are sold that he is credited with giving America a uniform language.

Boston's **Old South Meeting House** installs a stove. The *Evening Post* prints this lament:

Extinct the sacred fire of love,

Our zeal grown cold and dead,
In the house of God we fix a stove
To warm us in their stead.

Whether or not to heat churches becomes a controversial issue in congregations throughout New England.

1784 **Hartford** and **New Haven** are incorporated as cities.
The *Empress of China* makes the first direct voyage of an American ship to Canton, returning with tea, silk, porcelain, and spices. Sales of this cargo are so profitable that New England shipowners rush to enter the China trade. Maine ships that join in this long-distance commerce include the *Red Jacket*, the *Water Witch*, the *Flying Dragon*, and the *Black Squall*. Salem, Massachusetts, is the home port for many ships engaged in the China trade. Profits accrued in this commerce are the original source of the wealth of some of New England's most prominent families.

1785 The **Falmouth** *Gazette*, Maine's first newspaper, is established to promote separation from Massachusetts.
America's first **marble quarry** is opened in Dorset, Vermont.

1786 The **Humane Society of Massachusetts** is founded to aid shipwrecked mariners. This group will inspire the formation of the United States Life-Saving Service, which will merge in 1915 with the Revenue Cutter Service to form the Coast Guard.

1787 **Shays' Rebellion** increases support for a stronger federal government. In the so-called rebellion, Daniel Shays leads 1000 farmers in an attempt to capture the courthouse and arsenal at Springfield, Massachusetts, hoping to halt lawsuits for debt and to protest high land taxes. The farmers are routed by militia, but their desperate action succeeds in drawing attention to their plight.

1788 The new United States **Constitution** is ratified by Connecticut, Massachusetts, and New Hampshire; New Hampshire's ratification is the ninth and therefore causes the Constitution to take effect. In the ensuing election, George Washington is elected president.

1790 **Rhode Island** finally ratifies the new Constitution.
      Samuel Slater builds America's first water-powered cotton spinning mill on the Blackstone River in Pawtucket, Rhode Island, in partnership with Moses Brown. The machine-made thread is distributed to households in the area for weaving. Considered the beginning of the industrial revolution in America, the mills bring Slater fame and great wealth; at his death in 1835 he is worth $1,200,000.

1790-1850
      The **whaling industry** is important not only to Nantucket, but also to Newport, Providence, and Warren, Rhode Island, and New Bedford, Massachusetts. At first, whaling ships stay in New England waters, but by about 1820 it is normal for whaling voyages to last three years and to circumnavigate the globe. A popular route takes ships from New England ports to the Azores and the Cape Verde Islands, then around the Cape of Good Hope to the Bay of Whales in New Zealand. Whalers often call at the Hawaiian Islands for rest and recreation—the behavior of their crews is notorious—before sailing to the Bering Sea, then returning home by way of Cape Horn.

1791 **Vermont** joins the United States, the first state to enter after the original thirteen colonies. New York's land claims are setted by a payment of $30,000.

Salem has seven distilleries producing rum from molasses.

Portland Head Light is built, destined to become the oldest, most painted, and most photographed lighthouse in America.

1792 **Robert Bailey Thomas** (1766-1846) publishes the first *Farmer's Almanack*. Thomas, a bookseller, schoolteacher, and amateur astronomer, will publish fifty-three more editions from Sterling, Massachusetts (present-day West Boylston) before his death in 1846. The title becomes *Old Farmer's Almanac* in 1848; publication continues without interruption for two centuries.

1793 **Eli Whitney** invents the cotton gin, making cotton much less expensive to produce. Abundant cotton grown in the South and improving technology will give rise to cotton mills throughout New England and will create Northern interests favorable to slavery.

1794 Inexpensive **jewelry** becomes an important product of Providence after metal coating methods devised by Nehemiah Dodge lead to large-scale manufacturing.

The first **fire insurance policy** is written in Hartford, leading to the formation of the Hartford and New Haven Insurance Company, the forerunner of the huge insurance industry that grows in Hartford during the nineteenth century.

A **steamboat** is operated by Samuel Morey of Fairlee, Vermont, fourteen years before Fulton's demonstration of the *Clermont*. John Fitch steamed on the Delaware River in 1787.

The manufacture of **pottery** begins at Bennington, Vermont.

The **Springfield Armory,** the first federally-owned arms manufacturing facility, is established at Springfield, Massachusetts. Production of flintlock muskets begins the following year, and the operation is continuous until 1968. The armory plays a lead role in developing the "American System" of manufacturing, which relies on division of labor and increased use of machinery. The M-1 rifle, the basic infantry weapon of United States forces in World War II and Korea, will be developed and produced at the Springfield Armory. The armory is now a museum with one of the world's largest collections of weapons.

Bowdoin College, Maine's oldest institution of higher learning, is founded. Nathaniel Hawthorne, Franklin Pierce, and Henry Wadsworth Longfellow are future alumni.

Sylvester Graham is born in Suffield, Connecticut. Graham plays an important part in the vegetarian aspect of the reform movement of the 1830s and 1840s and publishes *Graham Lectures on the Science of Human Life and Bread and Bread-making.* His name becomes a commonplace because of his whole-grain crackers.

1796   Connecticut's **Old State House,** designed by Charles Bulfinch, is completed this year. The present Connecticut state house will be built in 1880.

1797   The oak-hulled frigate *Constitution,* 204 feet in length, is launched on October 21 at Boston's shipyard. Paul Revere rolls the copper sheeting that armors the sides of the *Constitution.*

     John Adams takes office as the second President of the United States, with Abigail Adams as his First Lady.

1798 **Eli Whitney** establishes a firearms factory at Hamden, Connecticut. This is one of the first efforts to use the principle of interchangeable parts in manufacturing.

1799 The **Peabody Museum** is established in Salem by sea captains seeking a suitable repository for items they have collected during their voyages.

    The **Peirce Mansion** is built in Portsmouth, New Hampshire, a classic example of Federal architecture, and one used as a model for many later houses. The centered front door is topped by a fanlight. Architect Charles Bulfinch was an apostle of this style during part of his career—Connecticut's Old State House is a Federal design.

1802 **Dorothea Dix,** one of the leading humanitarians of her age, is born in Hampden, Maine. She becomes an effective proponent of reform for asylums and prisons and is the chief of Union nurses during the Civil War.

    America's first **Merino sheep** are imported from Spain. By 1840 Vermont and New Hampshire have two million Merinos, which have heavier wool than the breeds previously in use by American farmers.

1803 The *Constitution* participates in the successful effort to suppress the piracy of the Barbary powers in the Mediterranean Sea. Commodore Edward Preble, of Falmouth (Portland), Maine, commands a fleet of seven ships sent to Tripoli.

    The **Middlesex Canal,** one of the first public works projects in the United States, opens water transportation between the Merrimack River and Boston, running twenty-seven miles through seven towns. The canal makes trade between Boston and New Hampshire more direct. The Boston & Lowell Railroad, built in 1835, serves much the same purpose and operates all year (the canal freezes during winter), causing the Middlesex Canal to cease operations in the 1840s.

Ralph Waldo Emerson is born on May 25, in Boston.

A **Vermont judge** rules that the only proof of ownership of a slave is a "bill of sale from Almighty God."

1804 **Nathaniel Hawthorne,** who will become famous as the author of *The Scarlet Letter* and *The House of the Seven Gables*, is born in Salem, Massachusetts. After an interlude at Brook Farm, (see 1841) Hawthorne marries Sophia Peabody. The first three years of their marriage are spent at the Old Manse in Concord.

1806 The Boston and Hartford Turnpike is built.

1807 In an attempt to avoid conflict with Britain, Congress passes the Embargo Act, which ruins American shipping but stimulates manufacturing. New England is badly hurt by the Embargo Act, and the following satirical verse is published in protest of the law.

> Our ships all in motion
> Once whiten'd the ocean
>   They sail'd and return'd with their cargo;
> Now doom'd to decay
> They have fallen a prey
>   To Jefferson, Worms, and Embargo.

The embargo was soon replaced with measures less drastic.

Poet **Henry Wadsworth Longfellow** is born in Portland. In his adult years he lives in Cambridge in the house that had been General Washington's headquarters. One of Longfellow's best known works is *Tales of a Wayside Inn* in which the Red Horse Inn of Sudbury, Massachusetts, is employed as the setting for a series of tales. Here is Longfellow's description of the inn:

A region of repose it seems,
A place of slumber and of dreams,
Remote among the wooded hills!
For there no noisy railway speeds,
Its torch-race scattering smoke and gleeds;
But noon and night, the panting teams
Stop under the great oaks, that throw
Tangles of light and shade below,
On roofs and doors and window sills.
Across the road the barns display
Their lines of stalls, their mows of hay,
Through the wide doors the breezes blow,
The wattled cocks strut to and fro,
And, half effaced by rain and shine,
The Red Horse prances on the sign.

1808 **Concord** becomes the capital of New Hampshire.

1810 **Cigar manufacture** begins in the valley of the
Connecticut River. Cigar-making had previously been a
cottage industry, a part-time occupation of farm wives.
Connecticut Valley Broadleaf tobacco is favored for the
outer wrapping of cigars, and demand for it is high until
the 1920s, when cigarettes capture much of tobacco
market.

The first **bridge** across the Connecticut River at
Hartford opens to the public.

1812 The **War of 1812** begins. New England dissents because its economy is based on shipping, which is halted
by the war. Before the war ends, New England's politi-
cal leaders meeting in Hartford briefly consider
seceding from the union.

The frigate *Constitution* defeats the British
Guerriere in a naval battle off Nova Scotia in August.
The *Constitution*, commanded by Isaac Hull, gains the
nickname "Old Ironsides" in this battle because it with-
stands the enemy's cannon balls so well.

1813   In waters off Maine's **Monhegan Island**, the British brig *Boxer* fights the U.S.S. *Enterprise*. The *Boxer* is under Captain Blythe, twenty-eight years of age, and the American commander, Lieutenant William Burrows, is a year younger. The two vessels are evenly matched. After hours of jockeying for position, firing begins. Blythe dies in the first minutes of the battle, and soon Burrows receives a mortal wound, although he lives to accept the surrender of the *Boxer*. The *Enterprise* tows the British ship into Portland Harbor. The whole city turns out for the funeral of the two commanders, and they are buried side by side.

1814   A new kind of **textile mill** is built on the Charles River at Waltham, Massachusetts, by Francis Cabot Lowell and the Boston Manufacturing Company, which raises capital through a new and controversial method—the sale of stock. The mill, based on British designs, is the first in America to perform all of the operations necessary for converting raw cotton into finished cloth. The company's labor force consists largely of young women recruited from farms. Success at Waltham prompts expansion on the Merrimack and the creation of the city of Lowell. An average mill family in the early 1800s makes about $650 a year, while the same family living on a farm makes about $180 a year but raises most of its own food.

   Abigail and John Adams celebrate their golden wedding anniversary.

   The **War of 1812** ends with the Treaty of Ghent.

1815   The **Handel and Haydn Society** is started in Boston.

1816   New England's **Year without Summer,** also known as the Poverty Year, the Cold Year, and Eighteen-hundred-and-froze-to-death. In the Connecticut Valley there is a heavy frost every month, with snow in June and drought for the rest of the growing season. The failure of crops encourages "Ohio Fever" for migration to western lands.

Maine attempts to secede from the Commonwealth of Massachusetts, but the United States Constitution forbids the division of a state.

1817 **Henry David Thoreau,** naturalist and author of *Walden*, is born in Concord, Massachusetts.

Ralph Waldo Emerson enters Harvard College. He waits on tables during the college year and teaches in secondary schools during the summer. Emerson is an early mentor of Thoreau's and gives the eulogy at his funeral in 1863.

1818 **Paul Revere** dies at age eighty-three and **Abigail Adams** dies at seventy-four.

1819 **Maine** votes in favor of statehood.

The principles of **Unitarianism** are set forth by William Ellery Channing, a liberal Boston minister.

1820 The Missouri Compromise gives **Maine** independence from Massachusetts, and Maine enters the Union as the twenty-third state. In order to maintain the balance in the Senate, Maine is brought in as a free state so that Missouri can be allowed to enter as a slave state. Maine's first capital is Portland.

1820s
Coffee comes into widespread use about this time, although it is derided by some as a dangerous drug.

1822 **Boston** is incorporated as a city.

Frederick Law Olmsted, environmentalist and landscape architect, is born in Hartford.

A **public library** opens in Dublin, New Hampshire, that has claims to being the first free public library in America, although Salisbury, Connecticut, had a free library for children in 1803.

1823 The **Champlain Canal** is constructed to allow boats to pass between Lake Champlain and the Hudson River.
Trinity College is established in Hartford by Episcopalians, as a theological alternative to Yale's Congregationalism. Trinity is called Washington College in its early years.
Formal **teacher training** begins with a school opened in Concord, Vermont, for this purpose by Samuel Hall.

1824 Poet, teacher, and editor **Lucy Larcom** is born in Beverly, Massachusetts. When Lucy is eleven, her father dies, and the family moves to Lowell. Lucy goes to work in the mill, but her education is not neglected. At twenty-two she moves to Illinois where she teaches school and continues her own studies. Larcom's *A New England Girlhood* is published in 1889. Here is the opening of her poem "By the Fireside:"

> What is it fades and flickers in the fire,
>   Mutters and sighs, and yields reluctant breath,
> As if in the red embers some desire,
>   Some word prophetic burned, defying death?

The first known **strike** in an American factory takes places at a cotton mill in Pawtucket, Rhode Island, after the work day is made an hour longer and pay is cut by 25%. The workers succeed in reversing the changes.

1825 The **Erie Canal** opens, connecting Lake Erie with the Hudson River. Cheap transportation of grain from the Ohio valley increases the difficulties facing New England farmers and gives New York an insurmountable commercial advantage over New England cities.

Along the **Blackstone River,** a canal is being built to connect Worcester with Providence.

The **ten hour workday** is the goal of striking Boston carpenters. Employers argue that so much leisure time would lead to dissipation and vice.

In Boston, **Quincy Market** is built, an example of the Greek Revival style popular in public buildings of this era.

1826 The **American Society for the Promotion of Temperance** is formed in Boston.

The manufacture of the **Concord Coach** begins in Concord, New Hampshire. This sturdy vehicle will be a standard means of transportation on the western frontier.

Boston's **Union Oyster House** becomes a public eating place.

A **lyceum** is established at Millbury, Massachusetts, and within five years nearly every town has one of these lecture societies.

The **Granite Railway** is built in Quincy to move stone blocks for construction of the Bunker Hill Monument. The distance from the quarry to the waterfront is three miles. In order to secure a right-of-way, the Granite Railway Company is incorporated by the legislature in March. The first train runs on October 7— pulled by a horse. The Granite Railway operates for forty years without ever using steam power.

1827 **Swimming instruction** is offered in Boston.

1828 The **Farmington Canal** opens, allowing boats to pass between Southwick, Massachusetts, and New Haven, Connecticut. Ten years later the Hartford & New Haven Railroad deprives the canal of much of its business, though canal operations continue until 1845, when a drought delivers the *coup de grace.*

1830 Poet **Emily Dickinson** is born in Amherst, Massachusetts.

The first American steam-powered **railroad** is built in Baltimore.

The *Constitution* is condemned but Oliver Wendell Holmes writes, in "Old Ironsides,"

> Oh, better that her shattered hulk
> Should sink beneath the wave.

She is rebuilt and returned to service in 1833, used as a training ship, later as a barracks. In 1934 the *Constitution* becomes a memorial at the Boston Naval Shipyard. Presently docked at the Charlestown Navy Yard, the *Constitution* is the oldest warship afloat in the world.

1830s

Old Sturbridge Village recreates this decade of New England life at Sturbridge, Massachusetts.

1831 In Boston, **William Lloyd Garrison** begins publishing an antislavery newspaper he calls *The Liberator.*

1832 **Augusta** replaces Portland as the capital of Maine.

Harvard student **Richard Henry Dana** interrupts his studies to take a sea voyage for his health. He serves as a hand on the brig *Pilgrim*, sailing around Cape Horn to California. Dana writes of his experiences in *Two Years Before the Mast.*

1833 A Quaker named **Prudence Crandall** opens a school for "young ladies and little misses of color" in Canterbury, Connecticut. The legislature passes a statute forbidding

53

schools for blacks. Before the question can be decided by litigation, a mob breaks the school's windows, causing Crandall to give up and leave town. Fifty years later the state legislature votes her a pension.

1834 The **Ursuline Convent** in Charlestown, Massachusetts, is destroyed by an anti-Catholic mob.

An **electric motor** is built in Vermont by Thomas Davenport and patented three years later, but there is not yet a market for electric motors.

1835 The **Boston & Worcester Railroad** is completed, linking Massachusetts' two largest cities. (In 1841, the Western Railroad will push the connection out to the Hudson River at Albany.) The Boston & Providence and the Boston & Lowell railroads also begin operations in 1835, and New Hampshire's first railroad, the Nashua & Lowell, obtains a charter. It is only five miles long, from Nashua to the state line.

Harvard Medical School admits its first woman student.

1836 Emerson publishes *Nature*, written at the Old Manse in Concord, Massachusetts. About this time the so-called "Transcendental Club" begins its meetings. Bronson Alcott, George Ripley, Margaret Fuller, William Ellery Channing, Henry David Thoreau, and Elizabeth Peabody all participate in this loosely-structured group. By promoting reform but defending individualism, the Transcendentalists help America adjust to the industrial revolution. As steel, steam, and the telegraph change the world, Emerson and his friends remind their readers of non-material values.

The **Bangor & Piscataquis**, Maine's first railroad, connects Bangor with Old Town.

Winslow Homer is born in Boston. He becomes famous for paintings made near his home near Portland,

Maine, at Prout's Neck, where in 1884 he builds a studio overlooking the sea.

Mary Lyon founds Mount Holyoke Female Seminary at South Hadley, which becomes **Mount Holyoke College** in 1888.

1837 Education reformer Horace Mann is given the leadership of the first Massachusetts State Board of Education. During the twelve years Mann holds this post he achieves substantial progress in public education and teacher training.

1838 **Putney, Vermont,** is the site of a new religious community featuring "Bible Communism" or "complex marriage," in which nonmonogamous sexual activity is permitted. Leader John Humphrey Noyes later establishes Oneida Community in New York on a similar basis.

1839 **Photography** comes to America. Francois Gouraud, a student of the French photography pioneer Louis Daguerre, arrives in the United States in the fall. The next year he trains several Bostonians to make daguerreotypes, and photography studios multiply.

The **"Aroostook War"** results from a conflict about the boundary between Maine and Canada. Troops from New Brunswick and Maine face each other across the St. John River until their commanders agree that the river will be the border, and tension subsides. The boundary is officially fixed in 1842 by the Webster-Ashburton Treaty.

1840 **Vermont** has six times as many sheep as human beings. In the coming decades wool production in the West increases, and Vermont shifts toward dairy farming.

1840s
>Railroads** expand rapidly across New England. In
Connecticut, railroad mileage rises from 117 to 551 by
the end of the decade. The New York & New Haven
Railroad opens in 1848, making it possible to travel
between Boston and New York by train.

1841 At **Brook Farm** in West Roxbury, Massachusetts,
George and Sophia Ripley initiate an experimental
community, and Adin Ballou starts the Hopedale
Community at Milford. To explain the need for radical
change, Ballou writes:

> Even the more advanced classes in church and state,
> seeking the progress, the harmony, and happiness of
> mankind, propose little if anything more than the
> *gradual improvement* of society on the old basis of
> egoism, caste distinctions, competitive rivalry,
> shrewd and cunning practices, jealousy and hatred of
> race and nation.

In the 1840s at least sixty communities around the
country search for a form of group living that will
improve society.

The whaler *Charles W. Morgan* is built at New
Bedford, Massachusetts, for $23,000. A hundred years
and thirty-seven voyages later she is brought to Mystic
Seaport in Connecticut and placed on exhibit.

1842 **Rhode Island** adopts a new constitution, reorganizing
representation in its General Assembly, which had become grossly unfair to urban areas. The change is
prompted by the actions of Thomas Dorr and his
followers who try to capture the Providence Armory and
set up a new Rhode Island government. Dorr is
sentenced to life in prison, but is freed in 1845.

In a pioneering **labor law**, the work day for children
in Massachusetts is limited to ten hours.

1843 In June, **Amos Bronson Alcott** and his followers and
family move to a farm they call Fruitlands in the town of
Harvard, Massachusetts, where they attempt to create
a completely ethical community. Cotton clothing is
rejected because cotton is raised by slaves. They do
not use leather, because cattle have a right to keep
their skins, nor wool, which they think should be left
upon the sheep. Eating meat is out, and although grains
and other garden crops are permitted, they are suspect
if the soil that grew them has been fertilized with
manure or cultivated with the labor of animals. Alcoholic beverages, coffee, tea, and even milk are all
scorned; their only drink is water. The Fruitlanders try
to wear only linen, the cloth made from flax, a crop
already widely grown in Massachusetts. Seeking a food
source cultivated by human labor, Alcott and his friends
settle on fruit—thus, Fruitlands, though their farm has
only a small orchard.

Preparations for the winter are entirely inadequate.
The community diminishes during the fall and has
perished by January. Unlike the other Transcendentalist
experiments, the duration of the Fruitlands venture is
measured in months rather than years, but the memory
of it is alive because its beautiful site and the original
farmhouse are preserved by the Fruitlands Museums.
One of Bronson Alcott's daughters, a willful little girl at
the time of her stay at Fruitlands, is Louisa May
Alcott, future author of *Little Women*.

Millerites expect the world to end this year in accordance with the prophecy of their leader, William
Miller. Many of Miller's followers give away their
property in anticipation of the end.

1844 **Charles Goodyear** of New Haven, Connecticut,
patents the vulcanization of rubber.

In Washington, D.C., **Samuel Morse** demonstrates the telegraph, which he has been working on since 1832.

1845 **Irish immigration** to Boston increases because of the potato famine. Penniless newcomers crowd into tenements in the North End, where they have a life expectancy of fourteen years.

Lowell, Massachusetts, savings banks hold $100,000 deposited by mill girls who work twelve to fourteen hours per day.

Henry David Thoreau lives at Walden Pond in Concord, Massachusetts, from July 4 until September 6, 1847. Thoreau publishes *Walden* in 1854, but it is little noticed before his death in 1862.

1845-55

Clipper ships rule the seas. The most successful of these large, fast ships are built at Boston by Donald McKay, whose *Flying Cloud*, launched in 1851, sets a record for the voyage from Boston to San Francisco; its elapsed time is eighty-nine days, eight hours. At first clippers bring tea from China; then they take forty-niners and their supplies to California.

1846 **Manchester** becomes New Hampshire's first incorporated city. In the decades ahead, Amoskeag Mills have forty-five acres of buildings along the Merrimack River and employ as many as 17,000 people.

Ether is used as a total anaesthetic in surgery by William Morton at Massachusetts General Hospital.

The **sewing machine** is patented by Elias Howe, Jr. After Isaac Singer and others perfect and mass-produce sewing machines, Howe becomes so wealthy that he personally finances a regiment of Union soldiers in the Civil War.

1848 **Boston** obtains more water from a pond in its western
suburbs. When the valve is opened a fountain of water
from Lake Cochituate shoots eighty feet into the air
above Boston Common's Frog Pond. In 1878 the upper
Sudbury River is added to the supply. The Wachusett
Reservoir is put into service in 1898 and the Quabbin
Reservoir in 1946.

Connecticut Mutual is America's first life insurance
company.

Samuel Colt comes to Hartford to build a factory to
make revolvers, which he patented in 1836. The
discovery of gold in California assures the success of
this factory, which makes 60,000 handguns in 1858.

Vermont finally gets railroads from Rutland to
Burlington, and from White River Junction to Bethel.

1849 **Maine** ships over five million feet of lumber to
California. The state's old growth pines are soon
depleted.

John White Webster becomes the only Harvard
professor ever hanged. He had killed Dr. George
Parkman and burned his body at the medical school.

1850 A national **woman's rights** convention takes place at
Worcester and proposes allowing women to vote.

The federal government's **Fugitive Slave Law** gives
rise to the underground railroad, a network of routes
through which escaping slaves are assisted in reaching
Canada.

The **chewing gum** industry begins when John B.
Davis begins making spruce gum in Portland.

The immediate success of Nathaniel Hawthorne's
The Scarlet Letter is partially due to its rather daring
subject matter--the scarlet letter is an "A," and it
stands for adultery.

Northern New England's big **log drives** on the Penobscot, Kennebec, and other rivers take place in the second half of this century.

1851 **Maine** prohibits the manufacture and sale of alcoholic beverages with a law that remains in force until 1934. By the mid 1850s all of New England is dry, but alcohol is legal again by 1868 in all states except Maine.

1852 At New Hampshire's **Lake Winnepesaukee,** Harvard defeats Yale in the first intercollegiate rowing contest.

1856 **Electroplating** of metal is invented at Hartford by Asa H. Williams and Simeon S. Rogers.

1857 The magazine *Atlantic Monthly* begins publication under editor James Russell Lowell.

The **coldest morning** of the nineteeth century is January 24, when temperatures reach fifty degrees below zero in Vermont and thirty below in Boston's suburbs.

1859 Educator and philosopher **John Dewey** is born in Burlington, Vermont.

On January 4 **deep snow** falls throughout New England. Hartford is buried by thirty-six inches, and Goffstown, New Hampshire, receives thirty inches in twelve hours.

1860 **Shoe workers** in Lynn, Massachusetts, strike for higher wages and union representation. The strike spreads to twenty-five towns and wins a raise but not a union.

1861 The American **Civil War** begins. The Sixth Massachusetts, the first full regiment to answer Lincoln's call for troops, rushes to defend Washington.

Ambrose Burnside is close behind with a thousand men from Rhode Island.

A wagon road to the summit of **Mount Washington** is completed from a base to the west of the peak. The Cog Railroad is built in 1869 on the mountain's east side.

1862 **Henry David Thoreau** dies of tuberculosis. Emerson's speech at the funeral includes this thought:

> He declined to give up his large ambition of knowledge and action for any narrow craft or profession, aiming at a much more comprehensive calling, the art of living well... He chose to be rich by making his wants few, and supplying them himself.

1863 A **Confederate privateer** disguised as a fishing boat brings the Civil War to Portland Harbor. The Confederates steal the lightly guarded Federal ship *Caleb Cushing*. They nearly succeed at sailing her out of the harbor, but the wind dies and leaves them at the mercy of steam-powered pursuit. Before surrendering, the Confederates scuttle the *Cushing*.

1864 At **St. Albans, Vermont,** the northern-most action of the Civil War takes place when twenty-two Confederate soldiers rob banks and flee to Canada with $20,000.

1865 The **Civil War** is over. Half of Vermont's eligible men served, and a quarter of these were lost.

1866 In **Portland,** a Fourth of July celebration starts a fire that leaves 10,000 families homeless.

1869 **Gypsy moths** escape from an amateur entomologist in Medford, Massachusetts. In the course of the next century they will spread north to Canada, south to Virginia, and west to the Middle West. In any given area their populations fluctuate; where they are numerous gypsy moth caterpillars devour every leaf from entire forests.

1871 Missouri native **Samuel Clemens,** who writes under the pen name Mark Twain, moves to Hartford. Twain's books include *Tom Sawyer, A Connecticut Yankee in King Arthur's Court,* and *Huckleberry Finn*; the latter is often considered his masterpiece. Twain collaborates with another Hartford writer, Charles Dudley Warner, on *The Gilded Age.*

One of Twain's neighbors is another famous writer, **Harriet Beecher Stowe,** author of *Uncle Tom's Cabin,* which was published before the Civil War and did much to excite public opinion against slavery.

Emerson takes a railroad trip to the Far West, visiting Yosemite and lecturing in San Francisco.

1873 **Earmuffs** are invented by Chester Greenwood of Farmington, Maine. Greenwood mass-produces them in a factory in that town.

1874 The Minute Man Statue by **Daniel Chester French** is placed at the North Bridge in Concord, Massachusetts.

1875 The original **baseball glove** is used by a first baseman for a Boston team.

New Hampshire's **White Mountains** become a popular summer resort and a railroad is completed to Crawford Notch.

1876 The telephone is patented by **Alexander Graham Bell** of Boston. The first telephone conversation takes place between Bell and his associate, Thomas Watson.

In April Boston's baseball team wins the first official game of the **National League,** defeating Philadelphia six to five.

Ivy league colleges meet at Springfield, Massachusetts, to discuss the rules for the new sport of **football.**

The **Appalachian Mountain Club** is organized in Boston to promote hiking and conservation.

1877 Boston's *Trinity Church* is completed in Copley Square. Designed in 1872 by famed architect Henry Hobson Richardson, Trinity Church typifies an architectural style called Romanesque Revival or Richardson Romanesque.

1878 The first **Columbia bicycle** is built in Hartford. By the turn of the century Columbia employs 3800 people and manufactures an automobile called the Columbia Electric Phaeton.

1880 As **deforestation** reaches its peak, the landscape of southern New England is nearly treeless. Farming begins a slow decline and the demand for cordwood falls as other fuels become available. Pastures and hay fields are abandoned and begin to grow back into forests.

1881 A **telephone** line is installed between Boston and Providence, Rhode Island.

The **Boston Symphony Orchestra** is founded by Major Henry Lee Higginson.

September 6 is known as the "Yellow Day" because the light is tinted by smoke from forest fires in Michigan.

The **last mountain lion** in Vermont is killed.

Clara Barton founds the American Red Cross, and serves as its president until 1904. Barton, born in North Oxford, Massachusetts, had risen to prominence as a nurse in the Civil War.

1884 The **United States Naval War College** is established at Newport.

1885 An **electrical transformer** is invented by William Stanley in Great Barrington, Massachusetts.
   Robert Frost, his mother, and sister move from San Francisco to Lawrence, Massachusetts. Frost becomes New England's most popular modern poet.

1888 A three-wheeled **electric automobile** designed by Philip Prate is built in Boston by the Kimball Company.
   New England is beset by a blizzard from March 11 to March 14.

1889 America's second **trolley** is built in Bangor, Maine— Richmond, Virginia, had one the year before.
   The **Underwood Typewriter Company** begins production in Hartford.

1890 **Refrigeration** still depends on ice cut from ponds during the winter. This year, Maine's ice exports total 3,000,000 tons.

1890-1914
   These are the glory years of the lavish summer homes built in **Newport** by wealthy railroad and banking families such as the Vanderbilts and the Astors. Bar Harbor, Maine, is another major summer social capital.

1891 **Basketball** is invented by James Naismith in Springfield, Massachusetts.

1892 **Charles and Frank Duryea** privately test America's first successful gasoline powered automobile at Chicopee, Massachusetts. The next year they run a more powerful design in public at Springfield. By the turn of the century the Stevens-Duryea Company of

Chicopee Falls is one of a dozen automobile manufacturers in the United States.

The **Church of Christ Scientist** is founded in Boston by Mary Baker Eddy.

1894 Town histories are published by many New England communities in this era. Henry Nourse, historian of Harvard, Massachusetts, writes:

> The locomotive has brought many advantages to the community, and also some false ambitions, morbid appetites and artificial tastes; and borne away much simplicity in life and manners without compensation in human happiness.

1895 At the YMCA in Holyoke, Massachusetts, William Moran devises the game of **volleyball**.

1897 The first **Boston Marathon** is won by John McDermott of New York City. His time is two hours, fifty-five minutes, and ten seconds.

1898 Boston's new **subway** is the first in America.

A tremendous **storm** strikes the New England coast in November. The "Portland Gale" wrecks 141 vessels, takes 456 lives, and rearranges the coastline.

1899 Half of America's **shoes** are made in Massachusetts.

In August, **Mr. and Mrs. F.O. Stanley** of Newton, Massachusetts make the first automobile ascent of Mount Washington—in a vehicle powered by steam.

1900 Half of Boston's population is **Irish** or of Irish descent, and only a tenth is of English ancestry.

1902 The **Mount Washington Hotel** opens at Bretton Woods, New Hampshire, offering lavish accomodations for 550. Amenities include a fabulous view of its namesake mountain, ballrooms, shops, and an indoor swimming pool. At this time large hotels designed to serve affluent summer visitors are thriving throughout the mountains of northern Vermont and New Hampshire.

1903 Baseball's first **World Series** is played in Boston. The Boston Pilgrims defeat the Pittsburgh Pirates.

1905 **President Theodore Roosevelt** meets with leaders from Russia and Japan in Portsmouth, New Hampshire, to negotiate an end to the Russo-Japanese War.

1906 The **San Francisco Earthquake** and subsequent fire cost Hartford insurance companies $18,000,000.

1910 The **Green Mountain Club** starts laying out the Long Trail through Vermont's mountains.

1911 Religious leader **Frank W. Sandford** predicts that the world will end this year. Sandford has gathered hundreds of converts from all over the world into a community called Shiloh, near Freeport, Maine. The group is known as "The Kingdom, Incorporated," or "the Holy Ghost and Us Society," or "Sandfordism." Sandford, who was a semiprofessional baseball player before he became a Baptist minister, buys a ship called the *Coronet* and sails from Portland to Jersusalem, where he takes aboard a passenger who later prosecutes him for detaining her against her will. Sandford is convicted and serves time in the federal penitentiary in Atlanta but resumes preaching after his release.

1912 A **workman's compensation** law is passed in Rhode Island to provide medical care and pay to those injured at their jobs.

Textile workers strike at Lawrence, Massachusetts.

Leon Leonwood Bean starts making hunting boots with rubber bottoms and leather tops. Beginning with $400 capital, he will build a giant mail order and retail business in Freeport, Maine.

1914 The **Cape Cod Canal** opens to vessels drawing less than fifteen feet. In 1940 the canal is deepened to thirty feet.

1916 The **Massachusetts Institute of Technology,** which was started in Boston in 1861, moves to its new campus in Cambridge.

1917 **John Fitzgerald Kennedy** is born in Boston.

1918 A terrible **flu epidemic** strikes Boston and other eastern cities in early September and spreads across the nation, killing nearly 500,000 people.

1919 **Acadia National Park** is established when Congress accepts a gift of land on Mount Desert Island, mostly on and around Cadillac Mountain, creating the first national park east of the Mississippi River. At first it is called Lafayette National Park, but in 1928 the name is changed to Acadia. Additional land, including much of the Isle au Haut, will be added to the park in the decades ahead.

1920s

The **textile industry** declines in New England as plants move to southern states. By 1935 Fall River, Massachusetts, has lost half its payroll and three-fourths of its textile industry.

1924 Even rural New Englanders are buying automobiles as the price of the **Ford Model T** hits bottom at $240, and Ford makes its ten millionth car.

1925 **Molasses** drowns twenty-one people in Boston after a storage tank bursts, releasing a wave of syrup twenty feet high.

1927 **Serious floods** strike the Winooski River, the Connecticut River, and its Vermont tributaries, resulting in sixty fatalities. Because the ground is already frozen, heavy November rains from a tropical storm cause streams and rivers to overflow their banks.

1929 *Birds of Massachusetts and Other New England States*, a monumental three-volume work, is completed by **Edward Howe Forbush** and published by the Massachusetts Department of Agriculture. Forbush dies on March 7.

1930 **Electricity** has been provided to only half of New England's farms by this date.
   The **Woods Hole Oceanographic Institution** is formed on Cape Cod to advance marine sciences. Because of its stimulating intellectual atmosphere and high level of interdisciplinary cooperation, Woods Hole is cited as a model research center.

1933 For her performance in *Morning Glory*, Hartford native Katherine Hepburn wins an Academy Award. She will win three more Oscars in the course of her long career.

1934 New England's **first ski tow**, powered by a Model T Ford, begins pulling skiers uphill at Woodstock, Vermont. Recreational skiing mushrooms in the 1940s, to the economic benefit of northern New England.
   February 9 is the **coldest morning** of the twentieth century in southern New England. In Boston and Providence the temperature is eighteen degrees below zero. On April 2, the highest wind velocity ever mea-

sured anywhere in the world, 231 miles per hour, is recorded at the weather observatory atop Mount Washington.

1936 **Tanglewood,** an estate owned by a Boston business-man, is given to Serge Koussevitzky as the summer home of the Boston Symphony Orchestra.
    In March, rivers **flood** throughout New England when rains melt a heavy accumulation of snow.

1938 On September 21, the **Great New England Hurricane** sweeps through the region, causing massive damage and killing 258 Rhode Islanders and more than 600 in all. At the Blue Hill Observatory in Milton, Massachusetts, winds are measured at 121 miles per hour with gusts to 186 miles per hour. Many, many trees are blown down by this storm. Along the shore, houses are washed as much as a half mile inland by storm waves.

1942 In Boston, the **Cocoanut Grove** nightclub fire kills 492 people in twelve minutes.

1944 The **International Monetary Conference** is held at the Mount Washington Hotel, laying the groundwork for postwar economic development. The International Monetary Fund and the World Bank are planned at the conference.

1947-48
    In the **snowiest winter** ever recorded for southern New England, Boston's snowfall totals 89.2 inches, and Providence receives 75.6 inches.

1953 On June 9, a **tornado** slashes through central Massachusetts, injuring 1299 and taking 94 lives in Worcester and neighboring towns.

1954 **Hurricane Carol** visits New England on August 31.

1955 Floods from **Hurricanes Connie and Diane** take eighty-two lives and result in a series of flood control measures, including the construction of a new dam at the mouth of the Charles River in Boston.

1960 Commercial production of **nuclear power** begins at Rowe, Massachusetts.

1960s
In this and the following decades, **agriculture** all but disappears in broad areas of southern New England. Former small New England towns that are within commuting distance of urban centers are rapidly suburbanized.

1966 The **Cape Cod National Seashore** is established in response to the growing demand for government protection of fragile natural environments.

1969 **Interstate 95** is completed across Rhode Island, and the Newport Bridge over Narragansett Bay links Newport with Jamestown, Rhode Island.

1970 By establishing the **Environmental Control Law,** Vermont takes the lead among New England states in protecting the public's interest in land use issues.

1979 Construction of additional **nuclear power plants** is prohibited by the Connecticut legislature, reflecting the controversy that has come to surround this source of electricity. Three such plants are already in operation in Connecticut.

1980s

As the **computer industry** reaches its peak of expansion and profitability, the region's economy soars, but by the end of the decade the boom is over.

1992 Despite the objections of Connecticut Governor Lowell Weicker, the **Mashantucket Pequot tribe** opens "Foxwoods," a casino, in the town of Ledyard.

Appendix

Milestone Dates by State

Connecticut

1614   Adriaen Block explores the Connecticut River.

1633   The Dutch build a fort on the Connecticut River.

1636   • Hartford is founded by Thomas Hooker and his followers.
       • Connecticut Colony is formed by Hartford, Wethersfield, and Windsor.

1637   The Pequot War.

1638   New Haven Colony is founded.

1639   The Fundamental Orders of Connecticut are adopted.

1641   New Haven Colony sets up a free school.

1649   Wethersfield builds its first ship.

1654   The Dutch are expelled from their fort near Hartford.

1662   John Winthrop, Jr. obtains a charter for Connecticut Colony.

1687   Sir Edmund Andros imposes the Dominion of New England of Connecticut Colony.

1701   Yale College is founded.

1732   Iron ore is discovered at Salisbury.

1754   Moor's Indian Charity School is founded.

1783   Noah Webster publishes his first spelling book.

1784   Hartford and New Haven are incorporated as cities.

1789   Eli Whitney establishes a firearms factory at Hamden.

1794   The first fire insurance policy is written in Hartford.

1796   The Old State House is completed.

1810   • Cigar manufacture begins in the Connecticut Valley.
           • The first bridge across the Connecticut River at Hartford open to the public.

1823   Trinity College is established at Hartford.

1828   The Farmington Canal opens.

1838   The Hartford & New Haven Railroad begins operations.

1844   Charles Goodyear patents the vulcanization of rubber.

1848   • Connecticut Mutual starts selling life insurance.
           • Samuel Colt builds a handgun factory at Hartford.

1871   Mark Twain moves to Hartford.

1878   The first Columbia bicycle is built.

1889   The Underwood Typewriter Company begins production.

1906   The San Francisco Earthquake costs Hartford insurance companies $18,000,000.

1979   The Connecticut legislature prohibits further construction of nuclear power plants.

1992   Pequots open a casino.

Maine

1602   Bartholomew Gosnold finds excellent fishing off the Maine coast.

1605   George Weymouth explores the Kennebec and St. George's Rivers.

1607-08
        Colonization is attempted at Popham Beach.

1609   Henry Hudson visits Penobscot Bay.

1623   Kittery is settled.

1629   The land that becomes Maine is granted to Fernando Gorges.

1636   Maine's colonial government is established.

1688   The Abenakis revolt.

1690   Portland is destroyed by French and Indians.

1691   Maine is absorbed by Massachusetts.

1702   Queen Anne's War begins.

1744   King George's War begins.

1745   Louisbourg is captured.

1774   Patriots in York destroy British tea.

1775   • Benedict Arnold leads troops up the Kennebec River to attempt the capture of Quebec.
        • The British navy destroys Portland.

1777   The *Ranger* is launched at Kittery.

1785   The *Falmouth Gazette* is Maine's first newspaper.

1791   Portland Head Light is built.

1794   Bowdoin College is founded.

1802   Dorothea Dix is born in Hamden.

1813　The British *Boxer* fights the American *Enterprise*.

1819　Maine votes in favor of statehood.

1820　Maine enters the Union.

1832　Augusta replaces Portland as the state capital.

1836　The Bangor & Piscataquis Railroad built between Bangor and Old Town.

1839　The "Aroostook War" occurs.

1842　The boundary between Maine and Canada is settled.

1850　Chewing gum is first manufactured in Portland.

1850-1900
　　　This is the era of big log drives on Maine rivers.

1851　Maine prohibits the manufacture and sale of alcoholic beverages.

1866　In Portland, a Fourth of July celebration starts a fire that leaves 10,000 families homeless.

1873　Earmuffs are invented by Chester Greenwood.

1884　Winslow Homer builds a studio at Prout's Neck.

1889　Bangor builds one of America's first trolleys.

1898　The Portland Gale causes widespread destruction.

1912　Leon Leonwood Bean goes into business.

1919　Acadia National Park is established.

Massachusetts

1602   Bartholomew Gosnold explores and names Cape Cod.

1605-06
     Samuel de Champlain visits and maps the harbors of Gloucester, Boston, and Plymouth.

1614   John Smith sails into Boston Harbor and becomes an enthusiastic proponent of Massachusetts colonization.

1620   The *Mayflower* lands at Plymouth..

1629   The Massachusetts Bay Colony is chartered.

1630   Boston is founded.

1635   William Pynchon and others settle present-day Springfield.

1641   The colony of New Hampshire unites with the Bay Colony.

1642   Massachusetts requires parents to teach their children to read.

1646   • John Eliot begins preaching to the Massachusetts Indians in their own tongue.
     • An ironworks is established at Saugus.

1652   A Boston mint begins to issue Pine Tree Shillings.

1659   Quakers are hanged in Boston.

1675-76
     King Philip's War.

1679   New Hampshire separates from Massachusetts.

1686   The Dominion of New England imposes royal authority.

1691   Maine and Plymouth Colony are absorbed by Massachusetts.

1692   Witch trials are held in Salem.

1702   Queen Anne's War begins.

1704   Deerfield is attacked.

1716   The Wayside Inn is built in Sudbury.

1729   The Old South Meeting House is constructed in Boston.

1768   British troops are stationed in Boston.

1770   The Boston Massacre increases tension between Massachusetts and Britain.

1773   British tea is destroyed by Patriots in the Boston Tea Party.

1774   Parliament closes the port of Boston.

1775   · The Battle of Lexington and Concord begins the American Revolution.
        · At the Battle of Bunker Hill, colonists prove that they are prepared to stand and fight British regulars.

1780   Massachusetts adopts a constitution.

1786   The Humane Society of Massachusetts is founded.

1787   Shays' Rebellion pits farmers against the government.

1795   The Springfield Armory begins production.

1797   · The *Constitution* is launched.
        · John Adams takes office as President.

1799   The Peabody Museum is established in Salem.

1803   The Middlesex Canal is completed.

1803   Ralph Waldo Emerson is born in Boston.

1814   A textile mill is built at Waltham.

1822   Boston is incorporated as a city.

1824   Lucy Larcom is born in Beverly.

1825   Quincy Market is built.

1826   The Granite Railway is constructed in Quincy.

1831   William Lloyd Garrison begins publishing *The Liberator*.

1835   Three railroads begin service from Boston.

1837 Horace Mann leads the first Massachusetts State Board of Education.

1841 Transcendentalists move to Brook Farm in West Roxbury.

1843 The Fruitlands experiment takes place.

1845 • Irish immigration increases due to the potato famine.
     • Henry David Thoreau lives at Walden Pond.

1850 A national woman's rights convention takes place at Worcester.

1861 The Sixth Massachusetts Regiment rushes to defend Washington from Confederate attack.

1876 The telephone is patented by Alexander Graham Bell.

1877 Boston's Trinity Church is completed.

1888 An electric automobile is built in Boston.

1891 Basketball is invented in Springfield.

1892 • America's first successful gasoline powered automobile is tested at Chicopee.
     • The Church of Christ Scientist is founded.

1897 The first Boston Marathon is run.

1898 Boston's new subway is the first in America.

1903 Baseball's first World Series is played in Boston.

1914 The Cape Cod Canal opens.

1916 The Massachusetts Institute of Technology moves to Cambridge.

1917 John Fitzgerald Kennedy is born in Boston.

1946 Quabbin Reservoir begins service.

1953 Worcester is struck by a deadly tornado.

1960 Commercial production of nuclear power begins at Rowe.

1966 Cape Cod National Seashore is established.

New Hampshire

1604   Samuel de Champlain sees the White Mountains from his ship.

1623   English settlement begins.

1629   John Mason is granted land that he names New Hampshire.

1641   New Hampshire unites with Massachusetts.

1642   Mount Washington is climbed by Darby Field.

1679   New Hampshire separates from Massachusetts.

1688   Abenaki Indians sack Dover.

1719   Scotch-Irish immigrants settle in Londonderry.

1770   Moor's Indian Charity School moves to Hanover.

1760-63
     The Hampshire Grants are made by Governor Wentworth.

1774   Sons of Liberty seize gunpowder from the British fort in Portsmouth Harbor.

1777   New Hampshire troops fight at the Battle of Bennington.

1808   Concord becomes the capital of New Hampshire.

1822   • Dublin opens a public library.
      • The manufacture of the Concord Coach begins.

1835   New Hampshire charters its first railroad, the Nashua & Lowell.

1846   Manchester is incorporated as a city.

1861   A wagon road to the summit of Mount Washington is completed.

1869   The Cog Railroad is built up Mount Washington.

1875   The popularity of the White Mountains as a summer resort is increased by the new railroad to Crawford Notch.

1899   The first automobile ascent of Mount Washington.

1902   The Mount Washington Hotel opens at Bretton Woods.

1905 President Theodore Roosevelt meets with leaders from Russia and Japan in Portsmouth.

1944 The International Monetary Conference is held at the Mount Washington Hotel.

Rhode Island

1524   Giovanni da Verrazano trades with Rhode Island natives in Narragansett Bay.

1635   Roger Williams is driven out of Salem, Massachusetts.

1636   Providence Plantation is founded by Roger Williams on land purchased from the Narragansett Indians.

1637   Anne Hutchinson and her followers buy Aquidneck Island and settle at Portsmouth.

1638   America's first Baptist church is founded at Providence.

1644   Rhode Island is chartered as a self-ruling colony.

1647   Colonial government is organized.

1658   The first Jewish immigrants arrive in Newport.

1663   Charles II grants Rhode Island a new charter.

1675-76
        King Philip's War brings disaster for natives and settlers.

1751   America's first snuff mill is erected at Narragansett.

1763   • Rhode Island College is founded.
        • Newport's Touro Synagogue is dedicated.

1766   In Providence, the Daughters of Liberty form to oppose the Stamp Act.

1769   The British ship *Liberty* is burned in Newport.

1772   The *Gaspee* affair increases anti-British feelings.

1776-79
        Newport is occupied by British troops.

1790   • Rhode Island reluctantly ratifies the United States Constitution.
        • Samuel Slater builds a mill in Pawtucket.

1794   Jewelry manufacturing becomes important in Providence.

1804   Rhode Island College changes its name to Brown.

1825   A canal is built along the Blackstone River.

1842   Rhode Island adopts a new constitution.

1861   Ambrose Burnside leads Rhode Island troops to the Civil War.

1884   The United States Naval War College is established at Newport.

1912   Rhode Island passes an innovative workman's compensation law.

1969   Interstate 95 is completed across Rhode Island.

Vermont

1608   Samuel de Champlain explores Vermont.

1666   A fort is built on Isle La Motte in Lake Champlain.

1714   Vermont's first permanent white settlement begins.

1760-63
        Land is granted to Vermont settlers by New Hampshire's governor.

1764   Britain places Vermont under the control of New York.

1775   Fort Ticonderoga is captured by Vermont's Green Mountain Boys.

1777   • The Battle of Bennington occurs to the west of the town.
        • Vermont declares itself an independent republic.

1785   A marble quarry is opened at Dorset.

1791   Vermont joins the United States.

1794   • A steamboat is operated by Samuel Morey of Fairlee.
        • The manufacture of pottery begins at Bennington.

1823   The Champlain Canal is constructed.

1823   A teacher training school opens in Concord.

1834   The electric motor is invented by Thomas Davenport.

1838   A controversial religious community begins at Putney.

1840   Vermont has six times as many sheep as human beings.

1848   Railroads open from Rutland to Burlington and from White River Junction to Bethel.

1859   John Dewey is born in Burlington.

1864   The northernmost action of the Civil War takes place at St. Albans.

1881   Vermont's last mountain lion is slain.

1910   Construction of the Long Trail begins.

1927 The Winooski and Connecticut Rivers flood.

1934 New England's first ski tow is set up at Woodstock.

1970 Vermont passes an Environmental Control Law.

Bibliography

Albion, Robert G, William A. Baker, and Benjamin W. Labaree. *New England and the Sea*. Mystic Seaport: Marine Historical Association, 1972.

Arnold, Samuel Greene. *History of the State of Rhode Island and Providence Plantations*, Volume I. New York: D. Appleton and Company, 1859.

Ballou, Adin. *History of the Hopedale Community*. Lowell: Thompson & Hill, 1897.

Carruth, Gorton. *What Happened When*. New York: Harper & Row, 1989.

Clark, George L. *A History of Connecticut*. New York: G.P. Putnam's Sons, 1914.

Cronon, William. *Changes in the Land*. New York: Hill and Want, 1983.

Drewry, Henry N., Thomas H. O'Connor, Frank Freidel. *America Is*. Columbus, Ohio: Charles E. Merrill Publishing Co., 1982.

Earle, Alice Morse. *Customs and Fashions in Old New England*. New York: Charles Scribner's Sons, 1904.

Fennelly, Catherine. *Life in an Old New England Country Village*. New York: Thomas Y. Crowell Company, 1969.

Finkelstein, Norman H. *The Other 1492*. New York: Charles Scribner's Sons, 1989.

Fiske, John. *The Beginnings of New England*. Boston: Houghton, Mifflin and Company, 1897.

Hale, Judson D. "To Patrons," *Old Farmer's Almanac*. Dublin, New Hampshire, 1992.

Hard, Walter. *The Connecticut*. New York: Rinehart & Company, 1947.

Harlow, Alvin F. *Steelways of New England*. New York: Creative Age Press, 1946.

Hemenway, Abby Maria. *Abby Hemenway's Vermont*. Brattleboro, Vermont: The Stephen Greene Press, 1972.

Howe, Henry F. *Massachusetts: There She Is--Behold Her*. New York: Harper and Brothers, 1960.

Howe, Henry F. *Salt Rivers of the Massachusetts Shore*. New York: Rinehart & Company, 1951.

Irland, Lloyd C. *Wildlands and Woodlots*. Hanover: University Press of New England, 1982.

Laska, Vera O. *Remember the Ladies*. Boston: Commonwealth of Massachusetts, 1976.

Laughlin, Clara E. *So You're Seeing New England*. Boston: Little, Brown and Company, 1940.

Ludlum, David. *New England Weather Book*. Boston: Houghton Mifflin Company, 1976.

Montgomery, D.H. *The Leading Facts of American History*. Boston: Ginn and Company, 1895.

Morison, Samuel Eliot. *Oxford History of the American People*. New York: Oxford University Press, 1965.

Randel, William Peirce. *The Evolution of American Taste*. New York: Crown, 1978.

Rich, Louise Dickinson. *State O' Maine*. New York: Harper & Row, 1964.

Robinson, William F. *Coastal New England*. Boston: New York Graphic Society, 1983.

Robinson, William F. *Mountain New England*. Boston: Little, Brown, and Company, 1988.

Simmons, William S. *Spirit of the New England Tribes*. Hanover: University Press of New England, 1986.

Simonds, Christopher. *Samuel Slater's Mill and the Industrial Revolution*. Englewood Cliffs, New Jersey: Silver Burdett Press, 1990.

Thomson, Betty Flanders. *The Changing Face of New England*. Boston: Houghton Mifflin Company, 1977.

Vaughan, Alden T., and Edward W. Clark. *Puritans among the Indians*. Cambridge: Belknap Press of Harvard University, 1981.

Wagenknect, Edward. *A Pictorial History of New England*. New York: Crown Publishers, 1976.

World Book Encyclopedia Chicago: World Book, 1990.

Acknowledgments

For encouraging me to publish *New England Time Line* as a book and for helping me put it in the hands of readers, I thank Dick Woodworth. For her steady support and editorial assistance, I bow to Cecile Costine, the best mother-in-law a writer could have. For reminding me how much fun it is to really sink your teeth into a project, I am grateful to Molly McAdow.

Mike Natale gave patient assistance with typesetting that went well beyond the requirements of his job, and the new cover reflects the educated eye of Bob Smith—thanks to both of you.

Information about New England history was provided by Larry Lowenthal, historian at the Springfield Armory, and by Virginia Spiller, librarian at the Old York Historical Society. The assistance of Elizabeth Dickinson of the Framingham Public Library, as well as the help of other librarians whose names I do not know, is acknowledged and emphatically appreciated.

The manuscript was read and corrected Francis Donovan, Cliff Hauptman, David Downing, Jed and Sally Watters, and Cecile Costine; it stands much improved by their advice. Jon and Ann Klein allowed me the run of their cellar, so that I could use Carly's nice Macintosh—thanks to all of the Kleins.

Index

91